Praise for *Happ*

'For a retailer, it's simple common sense: happy workers make for happy customers who put more money in the till. But happiness is actually fundamental to the success of every organization, from national governments to market stalls. Mark Price's book performs a great service in demonstrating how workplace happiness can be fostered and measured by all businesses, and the real difference it can make.' RICHARD WALKER OBE, EXECUTIVE CHAIRMAN, ICELAND FOODS

'A practical and persuasive guide on the competitive advantage that organizations can achieve with a happier workforce, brought to life by Mark Price's considerable experience. Against a backdrop of stubbornly low growth and a generational shift in what employees want from their jobs, *Happy Economics* provides the answer to a question many executive teams will be looking at over the next decade. Readers will come away knowing why employee happiness matters, what they should measure within their own organization, and how they can move the dial towards a happier workplace.' ANN FRANCKE OBE, CEO, CHARTERED MANAGEMENT INSTITUTE

Happy Economics

Why the happiest workplaces are the most successful

Mark Price

KoganPage

First published in Great Britain and the United States in 2024 by Kogan Page Limited

2nd Floor, 45 Gee Street   8 W 38th Street, Suite 902
London   New York, NY 10018
EC1V 3RS   USA
United Kingdom

www.koganpage.com

Kogan Page books are printed on paper from sustainable forests.

© Stour Publishing and Perry Ltd, 2024

ISBNs

Hardback	978 1 3986 1737 7
Paperback	978 1 3986 1736 0
Ebook	978 1 3986 1738 4

British Library Cataloguing-in-Publication Data
A CIP record for this book is available from the British Library.

Library of Congress Cataloging-in-Publication Data
Names: Price, Mark, author.
Title: Happy economics : why the happiest workplaces are the most
    successful / Mark Price.
Description: London ; New York, NY : Kogan Page, 2024. | Includes
    bibliographical references and index.
Identifiers: LCCN 2024024698 (print) | LCCN 2024024699 (ebook) | ISBN
    9781398617360 (paperback) | ISBN 9781398617377 (hardback) | ISBN
    9781398617384 (ebook)
Subjects: LCSH: Organizational behavior. | Organizational effectiveness. |
    Happiness–Economic aspects. | Employee motivation. | Job satisfaction.
Classification: LCC HD58.7 .P6874 2024 (print) | LCC HD58.7 (ebook) | DDC
    658.3/14–dc23/eng/20240606
LC record available at https://lccn.loc.gov/2024024698
LC ebook record available at https://lccn.loc.gov/2024024699

Typeset by Integra Software Services, Pondicherry
Print production managed by Jellyfish
Printed and bound by CPI Group (UK) Ltd, Croydon, CR0 4YY

Contents

About the author

Mark Price read Archaeology and Ancient History at Lancaster University and joined the John Lewis Partnership on their graduate trainee programme in 1982. The John Lewis Partnership's supreme purpose is the happiness of its employees. Mark spent 34 years in the organization, the last 10 running its Waitrose supermarket business and latterly also as Deputy Chairman of the group.

In 2016 Mark was invited by the then Prime Minister, David Cameron, to become the UK's Minister of State for Trade and joined the House of Lords as a Life Peer.

On leaving the Government he set up WorkL to help individual employees and organizations measure, track and improve their workplace happiness to improve performance. WorkL now works with over 1,000 organizations globally and, in addition, each week more than 10,000 individuals take the free 'Happy at Work' test.

Mark has also been Chairman of Business in the Community, Founding Chairman of The Prince's Countryside Fund (now the Royal Countryside Fund), Deputy Chairman of Channel 4, Chairman of Fairtrade and Chairman of the Chartered Management Institute.

Preface

Happy Economics is the study of how employees' happiness at work drives commercial and organizational performance. The quantitative data used in this book is drawn from the millions of WorkL 'Happy at Work' tests taken and supplemented by further insights from the more than 1,000 organizations WorkL works with.

Visit happyeconomics.com to see where your organization ranks on the global Workplace Happiness List.

Acknowledgements

I would like to thank all those who supported the writing of this book, and in particular Teena, Holly, Amy and our wonderful contributors.

But, I also want to acknowledge the brilliant team at WorkL who produced the data and work so hard every day to help people have a happier and more fulfilling working life.

List of contributors

TERA ALLAS, DIRECTOR OF RESEARCH AND ECONOMICS, MCKINSEY

Tera is Director of Research and Economics in McKinsey's United Kingdom and Ireland office. She leads McKinsey's research on the macroeconomic outlook, growth and productivity, bringing together deep expertise and more than three decades of experience in strategy, corporate finance, economics and public policy.

Tera is a thought leader, author, speaker and adviser on topics ranging from economic development and technology adoption to the future of work and corporate performance. She serves as the Chair of the Productivity Institute's Advisory Committee, a trustee of the Royal Economic Society, a trustee of the Productivity Leadership Group (Be the Business) and as a Governor of the National Institute of Economic and Social Research. She is also a member of a number of expert advisory groups on economic growth, productivity, innovation and labour markets. Tera holds an Honorary Professorship at the Alliance Manchester Business School, and is a Fellow of the Academy of Social Sciences and of the Royal Society for the Encouragement of Arts, Manufactures and Commerce.

Tera was previously on the board of Innovate UK, the United Kingdom's national innovation agency. From 2004 to 2014 she worked as Chief Economist in the UK Government's energy, transport and business departments and as Deputy Head of the UK Government Economic Service. Tera was appointed Commander of the Order of the British Empire (CBE) for services to economic policy in the New Year Honours list 2019.

YVETTE ANKRAH MBE

Dr Yvette Ankrah MBE is a transformational coach, consultant and trainer. She primarily works with high-achieving women to achieve success without burnout.

Yvette is passionate about ensuring people have the optimum environment, tools and skills to thrive. She believes that this starts from the inside and working in a way which builds sustainable and profitable businesses/careers without overwhelm, stress and burnout.

She has over 25 years of business experience, is an accredited NLP Master Coach and has a PhD in Sociology. She won a Microsoft/O2 award for business in 2013, was shortlisted for Best Coach at the Best Business Women Awards, 2015 and was awarded an MBE for her work with women in business in 2017. She is the director of Leading with C.L.A.R.I.T.Y., a corporate coaching, training and leadership consultancy.

She is a member of ANLP, the Coaching Society and the British Sociological Association. She is also a Coach of Excellence, accredited by the Professional Development Consortium.

PETER CHEESE, CEO, CIPD

Peter is the CEO of the CIPD, the professional body for HR and people development. He is also Chair of Engage for Success and the What Works Centre for Wellbeing and on the Board of the College of Policing. He sits on many forums linked to wellbeing, diversity and inclusion, routes into work and skills, flexible working and corporate governance.

Peter writes and speaks widely on the development of HR, the future of work and the key issues of leadership, culture and organization, people and skills. His book *The New World of Work* (2021) explored the many factors shaping work, workplaces, workforces and our working lives, and the principles around which we can build a future that is good for people, for business and for societies.

Prior to joining the CIPD in 2012, Peter was Chair of the Institute of Leadership and Management, an Executive Fellow at London Business School and held a number of Board level roles. He had a long career in consulting at Accenture working with organizations around the world, and in his last seven years there was Global Managing Director for the firm's human capital and organization consulting practice.

He is a Fellow of the CIPD, AHRI (the Australian HR Institute), the Royal Society of Arts and the Academy of Social Sciences. He's also a Companion of the Institute of Leadership and Management, the Chartered Management Institute and the British Academy of Management. He holds honorary doctorates from Bath University, Kingston University and Birmingham City University, and is a Visiting Professor at Aston University and at Unitar University, Malaysia.

LUKE FLETCHER, ASSOCIATE PROFESSOR IN HRM STRATEGY
AND ORGANIZATION DIVISION, SCHOOL OF MANAGEMENT,
UNIVERSITY OF BATH

Dr Luke Fletcher is an Associate Professor in Human
Resource Management at the University of Bath's School
of Management. He is a Chartered Psychologist and is a
member of the British Psychological Society, as well as an
academic member of CIPD, the UK's professional body for
people management professionals. His research interests
span both applied psychology and human resource
management and include topics such as meaningful work,
employee wellbeing, and diversity and inclusion. Dr
Fletcher has written for a variety of audiences, including
blog-style pieces for The Conversation and Harvard
Business Review Ascend. His work has been published in
several academic journals including *Human Relations*,
Human Resource Management Journal and *Journal of
Managerial Psychology*. Luke is a Senior Editor at the
Journal of Occupational and Organizational Psychology
and is an Associate Editor for the *International Journal of
Human Resource Management*. For more details, please
visit Dr Fletcher's staff profile at researchportal.bath.ac.uk/
en/persons/luke-fletcher

BELTON FLOURNOY, MANAGING DIRECTOR, GLOBAL
BUSINESS CONSULTANCY

In addition to being a Managing Director in a global business consulting practice, Belton founded his company's UK
LGBT+ group, which was awarded best LGBT+ network
in 2019 by the Inclusive Tech Alliance. Belton has also

been shortlisted as a Top 10 Inspiring Hero in 2023 by the Investing in Ethnicity awards, has been listed as #18 on Yahoo Finance's Top 100 Future Leaders, #15 on Yahoo Finance's Top 100 Ethnic Minority Leaders and was featured on the Top UK Black Role Models, presented by Google. Belton was co-founder of Pride in the City with Pride in London, where he ran a Mayor-backed initiative dedicated to increasing diversity and inclusivity across London businesses. Belton is also an Advisory Board Member for The Inclusion Initiative (TII) at the London School of Economics, supporting their innovative partnership programme bringing together research and practice to build more inclusive work environments.

He has over 15 years' experience in supporting clients with deploying strategic solutions across some of the world's leading financial services institutions, while maintaining a strong passion for ensuring diversity and inclusivity remain high on organizations' business agendas.

He is extremely passionate about intersectionality, where he believes it is each person's role to support other groups who are in the minority – 'After all, we don't want to preach to the converted, we want to educate and inspire people to be more aware and inclusive.'

ANN FRANCKE OBE, CHIEF EXECUTIVE, CHARTERED MANAGEMENT INSTITUTE

Ann Francke is Chief Executive of the Chartered Management Institute, the UK's leading professional body for management and leadership, with an international member community of over 200,000. She started her career at Procter & Gamble and has held senior executive positions at Mars, Boots, Yell and BSI.

Ann is an expert in management and leadership in the workplace and speaks frequently in the media and at conferences on this. She is a regular columnist for *The Times*. In the New Year's honours list 2020 she was awarded an OBE for services to workplace equality. Her book, *Create a Gender-Balanced Workplace*, was published by Penguin Business in 2019. Ann also authored the *Financial Times Guide to Management* and has been named in the top 100 women to watch in the 2015 Female FTSE Cranfield report. In 2023 she was awarded the inaugural Memcom Outstanding Contribution Award for her work in championing and acting as a role model in the membership sector.

GEOFF MCDONALD, KEYNOTE SPEAKER AND BUSINESS TRANSFORMATION ADVISOR, FORMER GLOBAL VP HR, UNILEVER

Previously the Global Vice-President of HR, Marketing, Communications, Sustainability at Unilever, Geoff is now a global advocate, campaigner and consultant in addressing the stigma of mental ill-health in the workplace and elevating wellbeing to a strategic priority in the C-suite. He provides a real practitioner's perspective on these issues.

He is a highly sought-after keynote speaker who inspires and provokes organizations to put wellbeing at the centre of everything they do, with a reputation for energizing and motivating audiences to take action in creating workplaces that enhance the lives of all employees.

His campaigning work has seen him participate in a number of BBC programmes and campaigns regarding mental health and wellbeing, as well as writing and producing articles for the *Huffington Post*, the *Financial Times* and HR-related journals. He previously convened a meeting at No 10 Downing Street with Prime Minister David Cameron and CEOs from FTSE 100 Index companies to address their role and agree actions to break stigma in the corporate world. He also provided some support to the Royal Foundation (The Duke and Duchess of Cambridge and The Duke of Sussex) in their mental health campaign.

Geoff has, over the last 11 years, worked all over the world and across all sectors. He is a Trustee of the Burnt Chef Project and The Baton of Hope, and acts as a strategic advisor to a number of companies with respect to elevating wellbeing to being a strategic imperative.

ANNE WILKINSON, CONSULTANT, WORKL

Anne Wilkinson is passionate about and supports businesses across multiple sectors in workplace culture transformation and enhancing employee experience. With a rich background in organizational development and human resources, Anne brings a wealth of experience, innovative strategies and friendly guidance to support organizations in making positive changes.

Introduction

On my first day working for the John Lewis Partnership in the UK, I was told that the supreme purpose of the department store and supermarket group was the happiness of the people who worked within the company. Its eponymous founder had figured out 100 years earlier that if his workers were happy, they would give more, staff turnover would be reduced, sick absence would be lower and customer service would be better. Add this all together, and the business would inevitably do far better than its less enlightened rival retailers. He was right, too. John Lewis's ability to deliver high standards of customer service has been the envy of the retail and even-wider business world. For the main part, the business has enjoyed sustained commercial success through the good times and through changing and challenging macro-economic conditions including wars, the internet and pandemics. The founder's vision has not stopped the business making poor strategic decisions, and on occasion has strayed from the founding principles to focus on cost-cutting and the bottom line. Whenever this has happened, its market share and profits have fallen. Yet, when the business returned to its underlying principles, growth and commercial outperformance followed.

My introduction to the vital role of happiness sparked a more than 40 year interest in this crucial business metric. Was it, I wondered, the key to success? And, if so, why? How can you measure it? Most importantly, how is it possible to create and maintain a happy organization? I realized quite quickly that I was not alone in my curiosity. For centuries, philosophers and thought leaders have been trying to unravel the power of this emotion. Socrates was the first to observe that happiness was attainable through human effort. He said there were two types of happiness. The first is the positive feeling we get from winning, or acquiring, something. The second is derived from altruism and the knowledge we've done the right thing, or done something well. This second benefit has a far more powerful and long-lasting impact than the first, he said. Both he and his fellow Greek philosopher Aristotle argued that all human actions were driven by their desire for happiness, suggesting that we can accomplish this, and that it should be a pursuit in its own right.

In 1968, Bobby Kennedy, when speaking of what made life worthwhile, said: 'We cannot measure national spirit by the Dow Jones average, nor national achievement by the Gross National Product'.[1] And, to build upon this, the psychologist Richard Easterlin demonstrated that, after a certain point, increases in national wealth were not matched by increases in happiness.[2] Both statements bring into question the widely held view that as long as we are all paid enough, there's nothing else to worry about. Life will be easier with money, yet without positive emotions it is all a bit worthless.

Fast forward to 2010, when I had risen through the ranks at John Lewis to become Managing Director of Waitrose and then also Deputy Chairman of the Partnership. I was working in my corner office on the fifth floor of the supermarket's HQ in Bracknell when my PA, Zoe, rang through to say she had No 10 Downing Street on the phone and would I take the call. It turned out to be one of Prime Minister David Cameron's aides. She was keen to know if I'd be willing to join a group the PM was pulling together to look into measuring national happiness in the UK. This would be an entirely new assessment which would take its place alongside the more traditional measures such as economic performance through GDP. The then Prime Minister had first mooted the idea of a 'happiness index' in 2005, when he was in the running for the leadership of the Conservative Party. Now, though, in the aftermath of one of the worst financial crises in a generation, he wanted to base his government's next steps on measures built on what mattered most to people.

He said at the time: 'The country would be better off if we thought about wellbeing as well as economic growth', adding that the measure could eventually 'lead to government policy that is more focused not just on the bottom line, but on all those things that make life worthwhile.'[3]

Having by then spent three decades with the John Lewis Partnership, working in both John Lewis and Waitrose and experiencing first hand the impact of the organization's supreme purpose where the happiness of employees was paramount, I felt well equipped to accept. I felt strongly that the notion of measuring national happiness was an important first step in spreading the word about the potentially huge uplift to be had by just thinking about the world in a different way.

Why did we fall out of love with happiness?

As everyone now knows, David Cameron's initiative was widely derided. The media called it woolly and impractical, while trades unions were convinced it was an electioneering tactic to somehow claim that the people of the UK were happier under Tory rule. The idea of a Happiness Index was quietly dropped when the administration changed.

What happened next is profoundly depressing. Following the media attacks, the mere word 'happiness' was apparently assumed to be so toxic that many organizations shied away from even mentioning the word. The corporate world, in particular, saw numerous organizations switch to calling it 'engagement'. Never mind that the phrase is completely opaque. If someone asked you if you were *engaged* in your job, would you have any idea of what they meant? It's hardly surprising that people are confused, not least because engagement has a wide range of interpretations from understanding the overall strategy, to being busy and working hard. It is, however, rare to equate it with positive personal feelings, unless, I suppose, it is in the context of preparing to marry a loved one.

Little notice was taken of the fact that 'happy' is universally used as a starting point for conversations on performance elsewhere. In sport, for instance, a coach might say to a golfer, 'Were you happy with that putt?' when they missed from 10 foot. A conversation would then follow about misreading the break, over-hitting, missing the centre of the putter face and so on. The question 'Were you happy with your performance?' is used on a daily basis as a starting point for an exchange of views. I can't imagine a waiter would ever ask, 'Were you engaged with your meal?' No, when asked if you were happy, this is an invitation to give specific feedback on why you might not be. The food was too hot, too cold, too chewy, or contained too much salt or pepper. By coincidence, this is the first step in understanding that happiness can be measured. It is not nebulous. Happiness is built on many factors, at home, at play and at work.

The sad truth is, many commercial organizations viewed happiness with suspicion long before David Cameron announced the initiative. If we wanted to dig into the reason behind the modern distaste for happiness, the Sixties should probably shoulder a lot of the blame. When the hippy movement advocated peace and love, insisting we should all be getting the most from our lives, it was seen as a little bit eccentric, certainly by older generations. Over time, the word 'happy' became polluted because it conjured a vision of laid-back people who had no interest in doing or achieving very much. Happiness came to be seen as the opposite of 'hard graft'. This negative association made it easier for a capitalist idea to take hold where it became acceptable for people to be seen as assets to be used by employers. They were paid to do their job, so it was a fair exchange, right? There's no need to talk about all that touchy-feely, fluffy happiness stuff.

Modern business has thus had a free rein to evolve to a place where, in its need to put shareholders first, those at the top of organizations see it as their responsibility to find the fastest route to maximize short-term increases in profits. I've seen organizations once famed for customer service decide to improve the bottom line by outsourcing their customer service departments elsewhere where labour is cheaper. There is a misguided belief this won't impact the customer experience at all and no one will notice. It does, and they do. It is a race to the bottom that ultimately fails. Yet, when it comes to profit, the belief endures that everything is up for grabs, as long as it is won via open and free competition without deception or fraud (in most cases). At a push, *at a push*, customer experience gets a look in as a useful metric, as it is now accepted that this is key to the longevity of any business. Disruptive organizations such as Amazon (mission: We seek to be Earth's most customer-centric company) have championed the idea that the customer is the most important person in the room. Many other businesses have followed this lead. But employee happiness? Until not that long ago, that's only been the number one consideration for a small number of companies. These businesses, such as John Lewis, Zappos, Innocent Drinks and, to his great credit, Richard Branson and his Virgin businesses, believe employees are the true custodians of the brand and drivers of customer loyalty, which leads on to better financial performance. These were, however, until recently the exception.

We are now, at long last, seeing more businesses beginning to tentatively embrace the opportunities of employee happiness, signalling a shift away from the idea it is a bit of a 'nice-to-have', soft measure. Said Business School partnered with telecoms firm BT, for example, to rate employee happiness for six months using an email survey with five emoji buttons to indicate states of happiness.[4] (The results were pretty staggering too. Workers were 20 per cent more productive in weeks when they were happy, versus when they were not.) That said, some early efforts to decode this happiness thing have been a little clumsy. We've seen a shift in the ubiquitous measure of 'engagement' towards 'wellbeing'. Happiness appears to have taken a place as a subset of wellbeing, albeit there is a growing recognition and acceptance that happiness does have an impact. This is, at least, a step in the right direction, and not a moment too soon either.

Workplace happiness is today more important than ever

In the 1942 film *In Which We Serve,* Noel Coward, who played Captain E V Kinross, opined, 'A happy ship is an efficient ship and an efficient ship is a happy ship. Invest in your crew – there are rough seas ahead.' That statement is particularly pertinent right now.

Globally, growth is an issue. The economic recovery from the pandemic has been slow and not helped by conflicts in Ukraine and Israel, supply chain disruptions and labour market pressures. Central banks across the world have been simultaneously hiking interest rates in response to soaring inflation. Emerging markets and developing countries have been dogged by a string of financial crises.

When there are issues with growth, it is a rare organization indeed that doesn't start questioning whether it is getting the most from its workforce. The first recourse from many company bosses, however, is to view the challenge from an exploitative standpoint around cutting costs. They ask themselves, 'Where can I find cheap labour?', 'Can I offshore this part of the business to India where it will be cheaper?', or 'Should we get our goods made in Turkey, and save 10 per cent?' What they're least likely to be thinking about is, 'Is our workforce happy?' (And can we help make them happier?) Are they committed? Are they engaged? Are they giving their best? Do my employees give more than my competitors' employees? But this is where the real competitive advantage lies. Those cost-cutting trade-offs, shifting the base of operations to far flung reaches of the world, are not solving the issue. (Not to mention the questionability of the practice that is not a million miles away from the colonial days of exploitation of developing countries.) By shifting operations further afield, companies might reap the benefits for 10 years or so, but they will then need to find another new solution. We're already seeing that the benefits of switching manufacturing to China or Vietnam are not as lucrative as they once were. Prices there are significantly higher than they were 20 years ago, and shipping costs are rising at a prohibitive rate, too. Ultimately, at some point, we will run out of cheaper alternatives abroad. Rather than looking to arbitrage labour costs around the world, everybody's going to have to retrench within their domestic market and think about getting more from their people. Forward thinking businesses should already be getting ahead of this trend and thinking about how to make their people feel happier, better trained, better informed and better looked after.

There is a greater urgency in some countries than others, and the UK would very much fit into the 'urgent' bracket. Growth in the UK has been static for 10 years. We also have an acute productivity problem that a succession of prime ministers have tried and failed to address. The normal response has been built around putting in more investment and better infrastructure. Here's the thing, though: no one (apart from David Cameron) has thought about happiness as the solution. In my view, it is no coincidence that there has been no recorded improvement in employee happiness during the period that growth and productivity have flatlined. In fact, it has probably gone the other way. If you look at the list of every country in the G7 that Britain is behind in terms of productivity, every single one is ahead of us in terms of the happiness of their employees. We are similarly badly placed when compared to the rest of the G20. We are significantly behind in some instances, too. The UK has a Wellbeing Risk score of 33 per cent compared with the US, which has a score of 26 per cent.[5]

During my 18 months as a Minister of Trade in 2016/17, I travelled the world and saw first hand what a massive difference a content workforce makes. Take Mexico as a case in point. The UK boasts a markedly better infrastructure and more sophisticated working environment than Mexico, yet productivity is higher in Mexico. Why? Mexicans are happier at work, according to the global statistics we obtain at WorkL. The culture is more familial and people feel like they are part of something. As a result, they work harder and are more committed.

That last point is perhaps key to the power of happiness in the workplace and why it is such an important metric. A manager's ability to get that extra discretionary effort from their people because they are happy and engaged in their work creates a significant competitive advantage and has a material impact on performance. It makes all the difference between whether somebody is prepared to take a call after hours and go the extra mile to get a project done, or just abandons it without a second thought and goes home.

When it comes to urgency, there is another very, very important factor as to why we need to focus on the happiness of our workforce: changes in the demographic. By 2030, 30 per cent of the workforce will be Gen Z (born between the mid 1990s and mid 2010s).[6] This generation, whose working lives have been changed by the digital world, the pandemic and shifts in working practices, has a very different view of the world. Older generations might dismiss it as all 'a bit woke', but for Gen Z their beliefs are sacrosanct. They believe passionately in equality and have strong views on how they should be treated, spanning their mental health, wellbeing and work/life balance. This might very well be because they've looked at previous generations and thought: we don't want to be like that. Whatever the reason, though, it is a challenge to attract and retain people from this generation. Surveys conducted by WorkL, the organization I founded to bring happiness to the workplace, show the lowest engagement scores for young people between 16 and 24. (67.3 per cent for 16–18 age group and 69.2 per cent for 19–24). Happiness is high on the list of priorities for a Gen Zer, though, with 70 per cent saying they would quit their job if they didn't feel happy. Throwing money at the problem won't work, either, with 72 per cent saying that satisfaction and meaning are more important to them than salary.[7] In less than six years, one-third of the workforce will consider happiness a *defining criterion* for accepting a job. If that doesn't make employers sit up and listen, I don't know what will.

Happiness and fairness will emerge as *the* most important business metric in the years to come, which is obviously long overdue. It will be for the one very good reason: economics. Or Happy Economics, as we call it. The companies that succeed will be those that prioritize the happiness of their team because, guess what, Socrates and Aristotle were right all along. When we feel good, we work harder and feel more disposed to the source of that positive emotion.

This book is a guide for businesses that are serious about driving productivity and improving performance. It shows how to measure happiness and then make a solid plan to improve the happiness score in the workplace.

I will say right away, this is about *employees* not customers. Customer happiness or customer centricity, whatever you want to call it, is of course really important. Every business wants to have happy customers, whether it's a newspaper wanting happy readers, or a chemical company looking for happy stakeholders. There are countless books on the subject (and I have written a few of them myself).

No, what we are laser focused on here is employee happiness. Although, it should be said, happy employees are key to making customers happy.

In this book, I explain how a focus on workplace happiness can drive commercial performance and why it's good for workers, managers, companies and the economy of entire nations. I'll lay out what drives workplace happiness and how it's measurable.

Let me share the magic behind Happy Economics.

CHAPTER ONE

The unrivalled power of extra discretionary effort

My first practical and tangible example of just how far employee happiness can drive commercial performance came in the early 2000s. At the time, I was Retail and Marketing Director at Waitrose. Historically, Waitrose had shied away from buying competitors' shops and pursued a slower-paced, organic approach to growth. The dawn of the first decade of the twentieth century presented Waitrose with an enticing opportunity for accelerated growth, as a number of food retailers became available for sale because many retail groups were being broken up under UK competition rules. This opened the way for Waitrose to buy small groups of shops from larger supermarket chains who had to divest themselves of part of their acquisitions.

Given the unique nature of the John Lewis Partnership, of which Waitrose was a part, there were justifiable concerns about taking on shops part and parcel with all their existing staff, as we were obliged to do under TUPE rules, where all employees are automatically transferred to the buyer. Would it, we wondered, create issues in delivering the high-quality Waitrose experience the company had built its reputation upon? The culture was very different at the stores we were buying and they all clearly had an operating model at odds with the one we were used to. The most glaring manifestation of this was some very obvious problems with staff satisfaction. One tranche of Somerfield stores, for example, recorded a staff turnover of 70 per cent and a 25 per cent level of absence due to sickness. These figures were very alarming and would inevitably have an impact on the commercial viability of the transaction. If the average store had 100 members of staff and the average cost of recruiting and training someone in retail was £3,000 this meant a single store was spending more than £200,000 just on staff recruitment each year. Hidden within those figures was a loss of productivity as successive new team members got up to speed with their new job. Meanwhile, management's time was spent sorting out the issues left by the absenteeism due to sickness and that cost a further £250,000 as salaries were paid to employees not at work. All the time that this staffing merry-go-round was going on, the service to customers was suffering.

The prospect of taking on these clearly ailing stores was therefore daunting. Waitrose had built its financial model on the standard metrics of store sales, property value and free cashflow. While we were fairly confident that our brand would be welcomed in various communities, we couldn't say for sure whether what we sold and how we sold it would be enough to deliver a bottom line ahead of what the original purchase price might suggest. Could we even make the acquisition viable at all? I remember thinking at the time that it very much felt like crunch time to prove the effectiveness of the John Lewis model of prioritizing worker happiness.

Despite the obvious risks, it was agreed that it was too good an opportunity to pass up, so we started to buy small parcels of shops. A strategy was put in place whereby, during the refurbishment of each newly purchased store, the inherited team of staff would be given three weeks training under a new senior management team who were versed in the Waitrose/John Lewis approach to management. They introduced the substance of our culture, explaining that it centred around respecting the individual on the team and thinking about their wellbeing and happiness. Meanwhile, the existing management team from the acquired stores was moved to branches in the original Waitrose portfolio for a more immersive training programme.

I admit, even I was surprised at how rapidly the stores were transformed. Within just three months, staff turnover fell to 18 per cent and sick absence to 3 per cent. As a result of this, there was a bottom-line benefit of £300,000 per annum, plus a marked improvement in customer service and efficiency. Why did this happen? We took active measures to engage the team, empower them and look after their wellbeing and personal development. They were proud to have joined the organization and, because of the way they were treated, the staff went the extra mile and willingly gave extra discretionary effort (EDE). As time went on, we used some of the considerable cost savings in recruitment to invest in staff training, which led to further improvements in productivity. We were happy to do that because we knew the investment in training wouldn't be lost to a competitor. This was a real life example of the stellar results that can be achieved through Happy Economics. I saw this happen in shop after shop after shop. During my time running Waitrose, we went on to take over hundreds of shops from our competitors. Not only did we get the sales benefits that we anticipated, but we also got exceptional service benefits from lower levels of staff turnover and sickness, and higher levels of experience and productivity. In turn, hundreds of thousands of pounds flowed to the Partnership bottom line, making these acquisitions far, far more profitable than even original forecasts. In fact, for a time, Waitrose became the most profitable supermarket in Europe.

The power of human capital

Anyone running a business is generally focused on three kinds of capital. The first is *financial* capital, which describes where they spend their revenue and how they spend it, because that gives a competitive advantage. Think here, say, of an organization that decides to invest all its capital on technology to improve customer service, rather than spending their capital on R&D to improve their products. Ultimately, the consumer will decide whether they want to shop in the business that's got better products, or one offering a better service. They have a choice.

The second equally important type of capital is *social* capital. This is the reputation that any business builds with its stakeholders. It is what contributes to what their suppliers, customers, the City (if applicable), the local community and politicians think of it. How is the brand viewed, and has the organization built that social capital to its advantage? These stakeholders do notice when communications are good, the brand is well thought of compared to its competitors and the team looks happy and is putting in the effort. It tells them that this is a great business.

The third source of capital is the one I believe to be the most important; it is *human* capital. The biggest difference any business can make is when it gets more from its people than its competitors are getting from their people. Now, in the old days, this was about: can everyone do a 50-hour week? How about 70 hours? Can we whip them harder? Historically, there have been lots of examples of the exploitation of labour. Even today, we see far too many instances of labour being exploited for the benefits of those that own the equity and the capital.

The downside of managing through fear is, in an environment like this, people won't stay around very long and will most likely take a number of sick days while they go for interviews elsewhere, or just compose themselves away from the office. A culture of performance through fear erodes an organization very quickly because of the high turnover of staff, not least because the benefit of their experience disappears through the door with them. Meanwhile, any organization that relies on the stick, not the carrot, will rack up recruitment costs. It may even become difficult to attract new employees as it gains a reputation for being somewhere people don't really want to work. The list of applicants will inevitably shrink, as will its social capital.

The Waitrose/Somerfield experience was a real demonstration that backs my fundamental belief that if people are happier at work, they give more extra discretionary effort, work harder and for longer hours. When people have a sense of ownership and belonging and they are happy, they work harder and are more committed. They'll take less time off sick, too, and be less likely to leave an organization. As a consequence of the latter, it is more likely to make any training experience stick and be implemented for the benefit of the business. Combine all this together and they'll also be more engaged with their work and will give better service to customers.

Whatever way it is achieved, ultimately, the success of virtually every business is based on whether the employees work better/faster or are more committed, even during 'off days'. When people feel happy, engaged and committed, they perform better. You could compare it to the difference between someone owning their business and thinking, this is my business and I'm going to work my socks off to make it succeed, and someone who does not feel quite as invested in it. If you can inculcate a feeling into the latter that they *own* the business and they're vital to it, then you will just get so much more effort from them. They'll want to give a bit more and they do it willingly. They won't mind staying on for that extra 10 or 15 minutes, or jumping in to do something that is not 'their job'. This is the secret to getting any organization to run at full capacity.

The success, or otherwise, of any business comes down to human capital. Is business A getting more from its people than business B? If the people in business A work harder, the company will do better. If the people in the rival company, business B, put in more effort, then business B will get better results. It is that simple.

If happiness at work drives economic performance and productivity, which in turn leads to a better working life for employees and better company results, this is further good news for the national economy, too, because it translates into increased tax revenues, which can be used to improve national services. There have been plenty of other clues I've picked up over the years, too, all of which have pointed to the fact that happiness is *the* crucial metric in company performance. The annual Waitrose-wide staff survey, for example, showed a clear correlation, (other things being equal) between its best performing commercial shops and those with the best employee scores. It is all about encouraging the team to give that extra discretionary effort. And, like workplace happiness, it can be measured too.

CHAPTER TWO

The facts

Measuring happiness

Despite the less-than-lukewarm reception of the Happiness Index initiative, my own fascination with happiness at work has never waned. In 2017, after I left the John Lewis Partnership and an 18-month period as Minister of State for Trade, I launched WorkL, a digital platform with one goal: to bring happiness into the workplace. WorkL tackles the task from two sides. On one side, we provide individuals/prospective employees with data and other insights into the happiest companies to work for, giving them the information they need to find the perfect job, in the right company for them. We also provide all the necessary tools to help them secure that role. On the other side, we work with employers, so they can measure, track and improve their employee experience and happiness, and recruit the best-fit employees for their business.

Measurement is, I believe, key to unlocking the potential of happiness. Businesses are usually very effective at measuring sales, production or costs, but, just as important (if not more so), is the need to understand how happy, or otherwise, the team is. If they are unhappy, we need to know why. Therefore, we need insights into the impact of all the various initiatives that go on and, crucially, to learn more about how much management is succeeding in driving higher levels of effort and performance from employees through maintaining a happy culture.

For some reason, before WorkL came along, it was perceived as 'difficult' to measure how different workplaces and leaders perform when it comes to happiness or driving extra discretionary effort. In the case of how good managers make their teams feel, these abilities were often (rather sneeringly) referred to as 'soft skills' which are intangible and therefore couldn't be measured. However, I consider them to be core skills, and their impact *can* be measured.

There is another, very pertinent, reason for measuring workplace happiness. It is very easy to *say* any variation of 'This is a great place to work.' Perhaps, those in the C-suite might even genuinely believe it. But is it true? Getting it wrong is not just sloppy and dishonest, it can also have some unfortunate consequences. When trying to attract the required number of recruits, it is not uncommon for organizations to exaggerate the benefits of working there. 'It's a happy, easy going office! You will love working here!' If this is not the case, or, indeed, is quite the opposite, the disconnect can be disastrous. Eager recruits will find the gap between what they're looking for and what they find is too great, so they'll quickly leave. This was exactly what happened with one call centre firm I worked with. The bosses were baffled by the fact the organization was seemingly unable to keep new hires for more than a few months. It didn't take me long to work out the issue. Upon investigation, it emerged that what had each successive intake racing for the exit wasn't just that call centre work is tough and relentless. What really grated was the shock of experiencing the gap between what was advertised and what it was really like to work in this unhappy workplace. Once these facts were known, the company became more honest about what the job involved during its recruitment process and closely monitored how new starters settled in. It also began collecting thorough data on exit surveys to help further refine its approach to working conditions. Within six months, it had halved staff turnover and improved productivity.

It is more than possible to delve into the happiness quota of any business. Today, WorkL collects employee sentiment data from over 100,000 organizations, both in the UK and around the world. The extensive measurements we use are based on a range of metrics. These include how well firms:

- fairly reward people for their labour
- recognize each individual's performance
- share information
- provide adequate training
- treat people with respect
- care for a team's wellbeing

- instil a sense of purpose and pride
- develop everyone's career
- build trusting relationships between those being managed and their managers

Companies using the WorkL survey not only receive internal insights on how the employees of various organizations feel but can also compare their score against competitors, marking them by industry and by geography. We also use predictive analytics to get a picture of the number of employees who are highly likely to leave in the near future and those that are a wellbeing risk and likely to take sick leave. We publish an index to show how inclusive companies are and another to show how well management is doing and whether they are getting the most from their team. Results can be filtered by a range of demographics to pinpoint where there are areas for improvement, as well as celebration. All of this contributes to our goal of encouraging a better working experience for employees, higher profits for companies, higher revenues for the government and a better society overall.

Using our data, we are able to see the happiest industries to work in (technology 77 per cent engagement score, financial services 74 per cent and construction 74 per cent), versus the least happy sectors (defence 66 per cent, retail 67 per cent and chemicals, mining and metals manufacturing 68 per cent). We can see the impact of the introduction/ withdrawal of working practices. We have, for example, been closely following the progress of hybrid and flexible working patterns, which first began to gain traction in the pandemic. While, as we know, these models have been embraced by much of the workforce, many people do miss face-to-face social contact. We also look at the attitudes towards pay, often an emotional subject, and the impact of salary on levels of wellbeing and the contribution to flight risk. Other significant factors that have an impact on employee happiness are concerns over recruitment issues and staff shortages, and a lack of training opportunities.

In Figure 2.1, showing engagement levels broken down by sector, it is possible to see the clear correlation between a high engagement score and lower levels of sickness absence and staff turnover. To further illustrate the point, in Figure 2.2 I've pulled out the rankings by industry, in comparison to where each sector ranks in terms of sickness and staff turnover. In health and social work, for example, engagement is below average, coming 11th out of the 18 sectors listed, and it has the highest level of sick absences (18th place out of 18) and is 13th when it comes to staff turnover. Those working in the professional, scientific and technical sectors are most engaged, have the least sick absences and are in the top three when it comes to retaining staff.

Our research has developed to such an extent that we can further improve correlations between the EDE indicators' predictive ability and a focus on either sick absence or staff turnover. One is driven by practical considerations and the other is more emotional. What comes across very clearly when you see these figures is that happiness is not just a nice-to-have, although people *should* be happy at work. The truth is: it's good for business, too. There are clear-cut economic benefits. Happiness *drives* commercial performance – and we can measure that too.

FIGURE 2.1 Engagement levels, by industry sector

	Industry sector	Sickness absence (Index)	Turnover (Index)	EDE Indicator (Index)	Engagement score	EDE score
A	Agriculture, forestry and fishing	70	70	70	71%	73%
M	Prof, scientific, technical activ.	60	92	76	75%	77%
S	Other service activities	76	94	85	71%	74%
J	Information and communication	70	106	88	70%	73%
K	Financial and insurance activities	87	96	91	74%	75%
I	Accommodation and food services	70	123	97	69%	72%
C	Manufacturing	98	98	98	69%	73%
F	Construction	92	105	99	74%	75%
L	Real estate activities	103	99	101	73%	74%
R	Arts, entertainment and recreation	76	127	101	71%	73%
H	Transport and storage	108	99	104	69%	73%
O	Public admin and defence	130	86	108	69%	71%
G	Wholesale, retail, repair of vehicles	103	117	110	67%	71%
N	Admin and support services	108	114	111	73%	74%
B	Mining and quarrying	130	95	113	67%	67%
P	Education	125	104	114	72%	72%
D	Electricity, gas, air cond supply	130	107	119	71%	74%
Q	Health and social work	157	106	132	71%	72%

FIGURE 2.2   Sickness and staff turnover, by industry sector

	Industry sector	Sickness absence	Turnover	EDE Indicator	Engagement score	EDE score
A	Agriculture, forestry and fishing	3	1	1	8	8
M	Prof, scientific, technical activ.	1	3	2	1	1
S	Other service activities	5	4	3	10	7
J	Information and communication	4	12	4	12	12
K	Financial and insurance activities	7	6	5	3	2
I	Accommodation and food services	2	17	6	14	14
C	Manufacturing	9	7	7	13	11
F	Construction	8	11	8	2	3
L	Real estate activities	10	9	9	5	4
R	Arts, entertainment and recreation	6	18	10	9	10
H	Transport and storage	13	8	11	16	9
O	Public admin and defence	15	2	12	15	17
G	Wholesale, retail, repair of vehicles	11	16	13	18	16
N	Admin and support services	12	15	14	4	5
B	Mining and quarrying	16	5	15	6	18
P	Education	14	10	16	6	13
D	Electricity, gas, air cond supply	17	14	17	7	6
Q	Health and social work	18	13	18	11	15

Extra discretionary effort (happiness in action)

When reading the Somerfield story, the naysayers might say that the chain had been run down for years and the staff were most likely buoyed by the fact they'd managed to hang on to their jobs. That's why they put in a bit more effort and were on their best behaviour. But what happened there was so much more than that – and the halo of relief can only last so long. There was no drop off in performance in later months. In fact, those ex-Somerfield employees performed just as well as their Waitrose colleagues in the years that followed, and the acquired stores went from strength to strength. Not only that, either. The same thing happened when Waitrose took over a tranche of Safeway and Co-op shops. This scenario occurred consistently with all the businesses that Waitrose bought from other retail chains.

While I had seen the evidence and results, I was aware that there would always be business leaders who might be cynical about this. Isn't it all a bit hippy-dippy? My experience of the negative response to David Cameron's initiative showed me that happiness was a tough sell to certain members of the media, business community and, strangely, even those in the workplace. While there are those who just instinctively think that making sure employees are happy is the right thing to do, there are others who need to see the numbers to believe it worthy of consideration as a credible business metric. They need to be shown that being nice to people and taking a bit more time to work with them is going to give a better result than just barking orders at them and telling them to go off and get on with doing the work. Therefore, the only option to demonstrate the powerful impact of happiness was with cold hard numbers. Enter the EDE Calculator! This is something developed by the team at WorkL to accurately measure the bottom-line benefits of a workforce delivering extra effort, or not, depending upon how happy they feel.

As the name suggests, the EDE Calculator helps to determine how much extra effort employees put in above what is expected from them.

How does it work?

We use company-wide surveys to ask individual employees to rank how they feel about working for an organization. The surveys are built around six factors that we have identified as essential for workplace happiness: reward and recognition, information sharing, empowerment, well-being, sense of pride, and job satisfaction. The questions are set out as statements such as:

I am happy with the hours I work.

I am fairly paid.

I am happy and feel safe with my working environment.

I have enough information and training to do my job well.

Employees are invited to give their answer to each one on a 0 to 10 scale. Thus, in the case of the first question here, if individuals are very happy with the hours they work they will score a 10, and if they are extremely fed up with the time in the office they will score a 0, or something in between. The answers across all the questions work together to build a picture that shows us how satisfied and engaged the team is with the organization and manager they work for. We then weigh this data against an organization's performance in the market, compared with the average industry performance. With data on more than 70,000 organizations we can see who is winning and losing against their competition and how much it might be costing them. Measures we look at include commercial performance and profitability, staff turnover, sick absence and salary. With these figures, it is a straightforward calculation to find out the potential return on investment (ROI) based on any measures taken to improve employee happiness over a period of time. The success of any remedial action taken as a result of these insights can be tested by subsequent surveys, and also against changes in the industry and among competitors.

For anyone who still needs to be convinced, let me share what our EDE Calculator shows when it comes to the link between results, productivity and the bottom line. When people are fully engaged, we see the result shown in Figure 2.3.

The EDE Calculator was developed alongside artificial intelligence (AI)-powered instant action software (IAS), so we could instantly give every manager results for their team, department or division, showing the top three areas to celebrate and three most pressing areas to address and make improvements to, along with the financial benefit of doing so. These remedial actions should occur immediately after a survey, and not months later when the data has lost its relevance. We further use AI and deep learning to produce heat maps that show results comparatively by manager, business unit, region, country, and across all job roles and demographics. The idea is to make it easy for any

FIGURE 2.3   The EDE Calculator

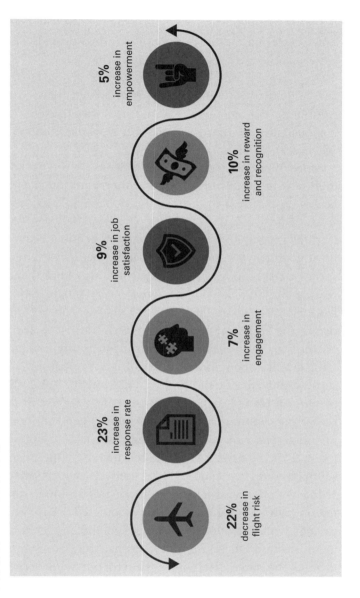

22%
decrease in
flight risk

23%
increase in
response rate

7%
increase in
engagement

9%
increase in job
satisfaction

10%
increase in reward
and recognition

5%
increase in
empowerment

manager to quickly and easily identify precisely where and how they could address any issues and to provide all the materials they would need to achieve that.

We have recently gone a step further, giving feedback and individual personalized plans to every employee who completes the survey. This means everyone can take responsibility to improve their own workplace happiness. We've seen spectacular results.

Since WorkL developed this measure, we have measured tens of thousands of organizations around the globe across 26 different industries. We've been able to demonstrate that there is a distinctive correlation between organizations getting high scores for happiness and a reduction in staff turnover and sick absence, benefits that flow through to the bottom line. Since we also know what it costs to recruit somebody across every single industry, from chemical manufacturing to legal, we can accurately define the true cost of a dissatisfied workforce for any business in these fields, and can identify any company's vulnerabilities compared to that of its competitors. We've seen employers put the EDE calculations to good effect, producing results such as a 22 per cent decrease in flight risk, 7 per cent increase in engagement, 9 per cent increase in job satisfaction and 5 per cent increase in empowerment. This, in turn, has generated income. One business services company with 2,000 employees which acted to reduce its previous high turnover in staff and high absenteeism rate is estimated to have created £826,000 in savings from introducing measures to encourage its team members to go the extra mile. Another technology firm of around the same size, which started out with very low engagement, was able to achieve an additional £617,000 in increased productivity by making a few adjustments to increase engagement.

Not only have we managed to definitively prove that happiness is a crucial metric in business performance, we have also compiled a rich database showing which are the happiest countries in the world to work in and the happiest sectors.

Building a business on happiness

If you accept that we have decisively proved the power of happiness – and we have – what is the point of continuing to measure it, you might ask. The simple answer is, knowledge is power. Things change in business all the time. If you don't know how, or why, or its impact on the most important resource, your people, then you are working with one hand tied behind your back.

Let me share the example of a large hospitality chain we worked with. The chain in question appeared to be doing well and was in expansion mode. When we first started working with the CEO, he appeared to have quite a handle on the figures. He told us that each time they opened a new restaurant, it cost £50,000 to recruit and train the new team. It was a clear line in the P&L and factored into the costs. However, after that it all got a bit murky. The sad fact was that once each venue was opened he had no idea about the levels of staff turnover or sick absence and their impact on productivity. Staff turnover is notoriously high in the restaurant trade, so it was a key metric. There were zero meaningful insights into whether things were going well or badly at individual branches. Using the EDE Calculator, we were able to determine the (not insignificant) ongoing cost to every restaurant of high staff turnover and then really get into the detail to compare the performance of one against another to show bottom-line impacts. We were able to say, this restaurant in location A has an issue with high staff turnover, high levels of sickness and, guess what, engagement scores are really poor. People are not happy working there. In fact, quite the opposite. Whereas this restaurant over here in location B had a really low staff turnover, very little sick absence and, surprise, surprise, engagement scores that are off the scale. The people at location B are really happy. And we could tell them why.

Information like this is gold dust. It shows organizations like this hospitality chain, with multiple remote outlets or divisions, exactly where it has management issues and where people aren't performing.

Armed with this information, the organization was able to focus on driving reduced staff turnover and sick absence as a key performance indicator and target poorly performing outlets. The cost of the exercise was paid back inside three months through improved performance, thanks to a much more happy and engaged team at *all* the locations.

The accuracy with which we can pinpoint problem areas can change everything for any organization because it means they can focus their efforts where they count. A separate great WorkL example came via another hospitality business we had been working with for a while. In this case it was a hotel group that had consistently scored very highly in earlier surveys. Yet, one year, their overall happiness score fell by 3 per cent. Now, that doesn't sound like a huge drop, and it isn't, but it was indicative of a potential issue that, if left unaddressed, could easily further erode the happiness score. When we dug into the numbers, we immediately found the source of the issue. The people who worked in the kitchen at one particular location, a flagship hotel, were really unhappy and that dragged down the overall score for the whole organization. With this knowledge to hand, the hotel management were able to concentrate their efforts in this department and find out why those team members were unhappy. Was it because they felt they were not being listened to, or did not feel they were being paid enough, or their efforts were not recognized? Why had they stopped having pride in what they did? They managed to track down the nub of the issue: a somewhat overbearing head chef. He was extremely talented, but had most likely watched one too many Gordon Ramsay TV programmes! Either way, there was a clear need for some coaching and development, and this is what happened. Problem solved and the scores picked up to previous levels the following year.

I should also emphasize that this pinpoint accuracy of measurement can be used the other way, too. It tells managers about departments where the scores are much higher than elsewhere. This creates an opportunity to find out more about the 'secret sauce' that's prompting things to go so well in this area and to congratulate everyone for such an outstanding performance.

There will always be organizations where leadership just don't want to know about issues in specific departments.

Their attitude is: 'Don't tell me! It's another set of problems I've got to manage.' But, by not managing them, they're generating even larger problems and, of course, impacting the performance of the business as a whole.

Some of the other benefits of understanding the Happy Economics of your own firm include better control of flight risk, improved wellbeing and greater inclusion.

Managing flight risk

Among the many measures we look at is the information gathered via annual appraisals, where employees complete detailed surveys and share results with their managers. We also learn a lot from new starter and exit surveys. These sources of information are invaluable for the process of analysing how people who were unhappy and subsequently left the organization responded to certain questions at the outset and then during their time with the business. As a result of doing this exercise extensively for some time, we can now predict flight risk among individual staff members with more than 80 per cent confidence, based on how they score certain questions. We know approximately when, too. Our data can tell with a high degree of accuracy that an employee is likely to leave within the next six to nine months. This information is highly valuable to any organization because it allows them to make early interventions to improve retention and reduce staff turnover, or build an accurate pipeline for new recruits.

For information, the UK had the highest flight risk scores in the globe in 2023, as shown in Figure 2.4.

FIGURE 2.4 Global flight risk scores by country, 2023

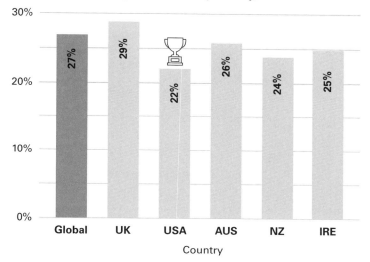

Improved wellbeing

Our data is also used to measure wellbeing risk, and identifies those employees who are most likely to take sick absence and who may, in many cases, go on to leave their job. This can be further broken down between male and female workers. Figure 2.5 shows the 2023 average.

Inclusion

Another area where we've put AI to good effect is in monitoring inclusion. The WorkL Diversity and Inclusion Index measures the difference in survey scores between majority and minority groups according to their responses to a number of core questions around inclusivity. The scale

FIGURE 2.5 Global wellbeing risk scores, male vs female, 2023

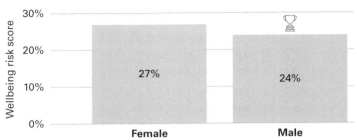

runs from −100 to +100 and a zero score showing a balance between either end of the scale being optimal. We can, for example, see clearly that disabled employees are less happy across the board and, perhaps hardly surprisingly, a greater flight risk (Figure 2.6).

Having all this information in aggregate is a powerful start in helping any organization improve. It allows businesses to understand where they are now and, over time, the data can be compared to year-on-year survey results, which shows how things have changed. (As a rule of thumb, we only recommend that companies do our surveys once a year. Any more and the team really does get survey fatigue. If a problem area is identified, there may be a call to go back and do a shorter, pulse survey four months later, to confirm the remedies put in place are working. However, anything more than that, we have discovered, is overkill.) Equally importantly, this process builds a picture of the industry as a whole, so it is easier to relate a business's performance to that of its competitors (from our database of 70,000 organizations across 26 sectors), to create relative and absolute performance indicators. However, the

FIGURE 2.6   Global flight risk scores, disabled vs non-disabled, 2023

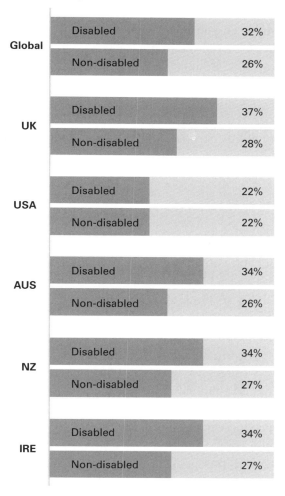

Flight risk score

most useful insights come from being able to view results on a granular level. If you have your head in the fridge and feet in the oven you might well have an average temperature, but you won't be in good shape! The real challenge lies in how that granular data is disseminated across multiple areas of the organization, by manager and by every demographic, and in identifying areas for celebration and those that require improvement. Most importantly, the objective of this exercise is to keep *everyone* in the organization happy, not just to spot and put out fires.

Using the data effectively

While much of this chapter has focused on what organizations and individual managers can do to improve their happiness levels, I firmly believe that it is every employee's responsibility to think about how they can improve their own happiness. Without a doubt 100 × 1 per cent improvements are better than 1 × 100 per cent improvement. To achieve that, organizations have to inform and empower *all* their workers to help them help themselves. When employees take individual responsibility rather than waiting for management to sort things out, this is what really drives productivity. A collective effort to improve is a powerful force.

To achieve this goal, the data gathering process and what happens next has to feel relevant to everyone. Coming from a supermarket background, where we had hundreds of shops, I am all too familiar with the scenario where the team begins to resent the multiple opinion surveys being carried out. More specifically, they were fed up that so very little action ever seemed to be taken off the back of the findings. When I used to visit Waitrose shops, warehouses and offices in the aftermath of our annual survey results being released, I would ask what they thought of them. The first problem was that the results didn't come out until about three or four months after the survey, so they'd almost forgotten about doing it. (I see this happen elsewhere a lot too. By the time management discusses the issue and lurches into action, staff have forgotten all about the survey, or voted with their feet in frustration.) The most consistent feedback, though, was that the results and any actions subsequently taken were so generic that they didn't feel relevant to them as an individual. When I thought about it properly, I could see why this might be. We'd presented the results as an amalgamation of the views, but we'd surveyed everyone from the 16-year-old who'd been there doing a bit of part-time work before they went off to university, right the way through to somebody in their early 60s who was close to retirement, and everything in between. It was impossible to reflect everyone's view. Meanwhile, in response to the generic across-the-board results, management would install a pool table in the break room, so everyone could relax more at break times. That was just not the right answer for the majority of people. Quite rightly, most of the team would say, well, what you are doing now bears no relevance to what I want.

Sadly, this experience is not unique. Research shows that over 80 per cent of employees think that nothing happens as a result of staff surveys.[1] Hardly surprisingly, they become sceptical of them. This leads to lower completion rates in subsequent surveys and so a spiral of irrelevance begins.

For this process to be effective, each individual must be given relevant feedback, as well as the managers. This will take the form of feedback and development plans personalized to *every single employee* throughout the organization.

One of the most obvious ways to do this is to use our survey as part of the annual performance review for each employee. Thus, before an individual has a review, they can take our survey and share the results with their manager. They can then discuss their answers and it is an opportunity for the employee to share whether they feel adequately recognized, or have the relevant information they need to do their job properly. By asking the right questions, people will be prompted to say; 'I don't understand why we are being asked to do *x*', or 'I don't think my views are listened to.' This strategic approach is crucial because it gets people talking about the right things.

The outcome of the survey also allows individuals to measure and compare themselves against people that look like them, of a similar age, gender, ethnicity and in the same job role. It will reveal areas where they may seem happier and more content than their peers and also where they're not as satisfied. Having information like this gives rise to a whole host of suggestions for what can be done to improve their individual circumstance.

Line managers can then work with their individual reports to set out a plan for improvement, and each person can be reminded that the next annual survey will measure performance against the plan to make sure everything is on track. What I really like about this approach is it acts as a constant reminder to everyone how important it is to be happy at work. The organization is making a serious undertaking to monitor happiness levels *and* will act if something is not going right. It also acts as a constant encouragement to line managers to do their job better on a day-to-day basis because it gives them pause for thought. 'Did I give that person good feedback just now? Or did I just bark an order at them?' Worse still, 'Did I say nothing as they left for the day? Did they therefore leave with the thought that this was another day of their life wasted?'

When employees at all levels get individual feedback coupled with a tailored action plan geared towards happiness, this is how to really drive the business forward.

PART ONE

Six steps towards workplace happiness

Imagine I told you that it is possible to achieve the following growth statistics for your business:[1]

- 20% better productivity
- shrinkage down 28%
- 41% reduction in defects

These improvements are all possible with a happy workforce. A 5 per cent increase in total employee engagement equates to a 7 per cent increase in operating margin.

As previously outlined, happy employees:

- are loyal – staff turnover is lower
- are healthier – take fewer sick days
- are happier – suffer less from stress in the workplace

Sounds compelling, right? But how do you achieve this? I used all my years of experience running Waitrose supermarkets in the UK, as well as that gained by sitting on numerous boards and visiting countless businesses worldwide as the UK's Trade Minister and of course my time building WorkL, to identify six elements that drive happiness and satisfaction at work, and therefore the engagement of employees, which in turn encourages extra effort.

Those six elements are:

- **Reward *and* recognition:** Pay is important, but *recognition* can be a far more powerful motivator.
- **Information sharing:** Openness and transparency ensure widespread understanding of objectives.
- **Empowerment:** Empowered employees have intelligent insights about how to do things better.
- **Wellbeing:** Happier, healthier people are better equipped to do business.
- **Sense of pride:** Pride in the workplace adds to a sense of fulfilment.
- **Job satisfaction:** A culture of trust and respect encourages a stronger bond.

We will cover the importance of each of these elements in more depth in the sections that follow, because each one has a crucial role to play in building the foundations for the happiness of the team. I've also included a few easy-win pieces of advice on how to make improvements in each category. These are all tried and proven techniques that are easily replicable elsewhere. Incorporating just a few of them would help any business be not just a little more decent, but more successful too. Better still, the benefits will flow to workers, communities and society as a whole. Later, in Part Three of this book, I will go into more detail to describe strategies to make more wholesale changes if any of the six areas has issues that are identified through surveys as significantly impacting the organization.

Most of the suggestions here in Part One require virtually no financial investment whatsoever, merely a change in attitude and approach. All that is needed is a new way of thinking. Get this right and it will build a sense of ownership around a business. Individuals on the team who feel they have more power over their working life, wellbeing and environment will take more responsibility for the success of their employer, choosing to expend that all-important extra discretionary effort.

CHAPTER THREE

Reward and recognition

In the world of work, it's all about the money, right? We're all in it for the big bucks. Well, yes and no. When it comes to happiness and engagement, the picture is less black and white.

Compensation is important because we've all got bills to pay. Plus, salaries have to be competitive to attract and retain employees. However, it is the non-financial factors such as recognition that really moves the dial when it comes to motivating people in their jobs.

There are a lot of myths about pay, so let's clear a few of them up before we talk about recognition and why this is so important. The first centres around how we benchmark our compensation. No one sits in an office and thinks: 'Emma Stone earns hundreds of millions doing movies. That's not fair, I should get that.' It would be a nonsense to compare ourselves to a Hollywood actor in terms of pay. What we do, though, is compare ourselves and our pay to what other people on a similar level in our sector earn. We have a benchmark that we think is fair. Once we've settled upon that benchmark, we then either feel happy, or less happy, if we are under or over that particular score, even if it is just by a small amount.

I have first-hand experience of this. In my younger years, working for John Lewis at a time when inflation was running pretty high at around 13 per cent, I was awarded a 10 per cent pay increase at my annual review and was very unhappy about it indeed. I can still distinctly remember the conversation I had with my managing director at the time. I told him straight out that I believed 15 per cent would have been fair. Yes, my ask represented a huge percentage raise, but what I had been offered undercut what everybody else seemed to be getting. Being slightly under – in my case 3 per cent under the inflation figure – I felt aggrieved. It niggled at me. If they had paid me 2 per cent above, I'd have probably been happy. This taught me an important lesson. Pay only ever *mitigates discontent*. Pay in and of itself does not drive performance. This chimes with Frederick Herzberg's theory of motivation in the workplace. The renowned business management psychologist said that pay and working conditions can only ever minimize dissatisfaction with work. Neither pay nor working conditions are enough to promote satisfaction or engagement on their own merits. Responsibility, achievement, recognition, type of work and potential for advancement are far more important sources of motivation.

I should add, those who work in the sales environment are the exception to this rule. They appear to have a certain mindset where they resolve to work 24/7 until they earn millions in bonuses and are completely driven by that. That's a particular set of individuals, though. The vast majority of people who do jobs that they enjoy are not necessarily driven by wanting to earn huge amounts, although they do want to be fairly paid.

Something else that really concerns individuals about their pay rate is that it should reflect their contribution to the business. Financial rewards for discretionary effort does make a huge difference to motivation levels. It always amazes me when I come across firms where everybody doing the 'same job' is paid at an identical rate. How can that be right when it is almost impossible that each person on the team is putting in the same energy and effort? It is inevitable that this equal pay structure will cause resentment. Think about it. If everybody is paid, say, £20 an hour, what about Tim, who constantly disappears for 20-minute tea breaks, at least six times a day? Or Rupa, who can be found working diligently at her desk an hour before her colleagues arrive each day and long after many have left in the afternoon? Should they both be paid at an identical rate? It doesn't seem fair reading it here and, rest assured, it won't seem fair to Rupa. It is far better to declare that £20 an hour is the *average* rate of pay in the department. It is then at the manager's discretion to go above that for those on the team putting in extra and a little below for those who give less. The better colleagues perform, the better the compensation. As well as the all-important recognition factor that is tied into pay levels, this drives commercial performance for the benefit of all.

It should, of course, be said that this strategy stands or falls by the robustness of the line manager's performance reviews and the measurements they use to assess the team. It might be that the apparently workshy Tim is, in fact, helping a colleague elsewhere in the business. Perhaps his true calling lies in tech and he is hanging out with the IT team to lend a hand on a project that is not going as it should. His intervention there might be invaluable. In which case, docking him £2 an hour does not seem as reasonable as it might have done at first sight. Although in this case, it might also seem sensible to consider reassigning him to another department.

Recognition trumps reward

The ability of a manager to notice what people are doing and to acknowledge their good work is critical to whether people are happy in their work, far more so than financial reward. Everybody wants to be recognized for doing something well. As per Maslow's hierarchy of needs, two of the most important psychological needs are the desire to be *appreciated* and to *belong*. Saying thank you, or congratulations, for a job well done goes a long way.

If you want to understand why Americans score much better in the workplace happiness stakes than the British (75 per cent and 69 per cent respectively), I'd say a great deal is down to the fact that it is the norm in US firms to praise their people *every day*. A cynic might suggest that

FIGURE 3.1   The responses to the WorkL survey on the importance of reward and recognition, by age group. The higher the number, the happier this age is with their reward and recognition

Age	Reward and recognition
19–24	68%
25–34	69%
35–44	71%
45–54	71%
55–64	71%

FIGURE 3.2   The WorkL survey, broken down by ethnicity

Ethnicity	Reward and recognition
Arab	69%
Asian/Asian British	71%
Black/African/Caribbean/Black British	71%
Mixed/Multiple ethnic groups	67%
Other ethnic group	71%
Prefer not to say	66%
White	70%

clapping and saying 'Good job!' is fake and sounds insincere, but it works and has a noticeable impact on happiness levels. Managers at British firms don't generally do this. On average, we praise people, or give them positive feedback, twice every quarter. Meanwhile, we give them constructive feedback (aka moan about their performance) *at least* a couple of times a week. It's not in our culture to give credit where it is due, certainly not on a regular basis. Yet when individuals on our teams rarely hear what they are doing right, it is inevitable they feel that they're not doing things well.

How do you get over the cynicism? Well, the praise has to be real. Businesses only thrive when its management and leadership are *genuinely* interested. If a line manager is attentive to their reports and constantly checks in, it makes a difference. It's not difficult to achieve. The conversation can be started by asking:

'How's it going?'

'What are you working on?'

'Is there anything you need help with?'

If these conversations are had on a regular basis, team members will see that their managers are taking a real interest in them and their achievements. This is a no-cost improvement that will make an outsized difference. Too many managers just don't care. They think that their team is there to serve them, not that they are there to serve their teams, or that the number one purpose of their teams is to make them look good. The team is there to *help them* do a brilliant job. That difference in emphasis is crucial.

If there is any budget, spending a small amount on recognition can be very cost-effective. Structured reward and recognition programmes can have a big impact. In the annual *Sunday Times* Best Places to Work, which WorkL runs on the newspaper's behalf, one of the factors that unites the highest rated companies every time is that they always invest in such programmes. I am also very keen on any 'random act of kindness' schemes that encourage spontaneous awards for staff who do more than is asked. We introduced the 'one step beyond' scheme at Waitrose, where managers were given a 'cheque book' where they could instantly write out a reward to a staff member for a job well done. The award could be a dinner, day away with the family, or tickets to a sports event, or alternatively the manager could hand out wine, flowers or chocolates. We trusted them to make their own decisions, so there was not a huge wait while things were signed off. The programme was hugely effective. It was a simple way for managers to show they cared and noticed someone's contribution on an ongoing basis. It's so much better to acknowledge extra discretionary effort in real time, rather than just once a year at pay review time.

For a business to flourish, the most senior management must take a real interest in everybody on a day-to-day basis. Everybody should feel that they are noticed and they're important. If any team member is left thinking, 'I'm doing this year after year and nobody ever tells me I've done a good job', it is dreadful. It's a psychological burden and is undoubtedly a contributing factor towards why we have high rates of anxiety and depression in the workplace, particularly among young people. They're working hard, but never even see their managers, let alone be acknowledged or rewarded. They're not being encouraged day to day or being helped to develop. It's inevitable that this leads to issues with wellbeing and drives down energy levels, all of which are to the detriment of the business.

Starting the conversation

Anyone who still harbours concerns about sounding insincere should think about ways that they can start a conversation to create a regular rapport with team members. I'll give an example here from something that happened during my time running Waitrose.

As anyone familiar with retail will no doubt know, gondola ends are hugely important areas in any store. These are the areas at the end of each aisle of shelves which every shopper passes and therefore enjoy the highest rates of sales out of the whole store. This is why supermarkets feature their most compelling promotions on gondola ends and manufacturing suppliers and big brands pay top dollar just to get some space in this prestigious area.

I was on a visit to a particular store and on a walka-round with the store manager when I noticed, to my surprise, that one of the gondola ends was completely empty. There was not a single product on the shelves of this valuable part of retail real estate. When I pointed this out to the manager, he looked quite irritated and immediately beckoned over a sales assistant. I can't remember his exact words to the young lad, but it was something along the lines of: 'Oi, get these shelves filled, pronto.' I watched as the lad wandered off in the direction of the stock room to get the boxes to fill the gondola end. His shoulders were slumped and he was a picture of despondency.

I would, I explained to the manager, have tackled that situation very differently. I'd have said to him something along the lines of: 'Do you realize how important that gondola end is to our commercial success? I am not sure if you realize it, but we take an average of £1,000 in sales every day from this area. Over the course of a week, that gondola end will be responsible for 5 per cent of the total turnover of the shop and you are the person that's responsible for it. You have the responsibility to make sure that we maximize those sales. Our commercial success is in large part down to you. We can be up 5 per cent or down 5 per cent, as a result of your contribution.'

I would have then followed this up by telling the sales assistant that I (in the role of his line manager) wanted to make sure he was supported in keeping that gondola end full. Thus, every day, the manager should share details of the previous day's sales on those shelves and give proper feedback to his young report.

If the manager did this, he'd be able to go to this lad every day and say, 'You did a brilliant job, Freddie. Yesterday, we made £x amount of sales on this gondola and it was never out of stock. Thank you very much for what you've done.'

That's the difference. It's that simple. In any situation like this, the manager could either just say, 'Go and fill the shelf, you idiot,' or they could explain to their team member why the role that they play is so important. Then, once they've opened that dialogue, they can notice and acknowledge the effort being made.

There are two crucial actions going on here. One is where a manager genuinely wants to know how their team members are getting on and make them feel involved. The second is helping them feel proud of the organization they work for and that they have a role to play in its commercial success. That's where the US performs so much better than the UK does, and why US teams are happier. Their workers feel consistently more recognized when they do something well. In the UK, they don't because senior staff aren't taking much interest.

Employees want to feel 'seen' and valued. Taking just a few moments *every day* to give positive feedback, whether in a formal way as part of a recognition programme, or simply giving a verbal thank you, or a handwritten note, is meaningful and does have an impact. It's also hugely motivating.

CHAPTER FOUR

Information sharing

One of my earliest jobs with the John Lewis Partnership was as a section manager in the garden furniture department of Tyrrell and Green in Southampton. This is one of the most junior management positions and I'd not been there long when a customer arrived with a complaint about a parasol he'd bought from us which had broken not long after he'd taken it home. After a brief conversation, I quickly established that it needed a new part.

I reassured the customer that I would get onto the issue right away and, while he was still there in the store, I filled in the requisite form to order the replacement part. As soon as he left, I dropped it into the office myself.

I didn't think much more about the matter, confident that, since I had gone through the right procedure, the customer would probably be sitting in the shade of his newly repaired parasol within a matter of days. I was wrong. One month later, the customer returned and, after one look at his face, I knew before he'd even spoken that nothing had happened. Sure enough, it turned out that he had not yet heard from us, let alone received the part.

I reassured him that the situation was highly unusual and said I would go to the office straight away to find out what had happened. This is exactly what I duly did.

'Did you fill out the form?' the person in the office asked, in response to my enquiry.

'I did,' I said.

'Then, don't worry about it,' came the reply. 'It'll be fine.'

To cut a long story short, this went on for about three months, with the customer getting more and more frustrated each time he appeared in the garden furniture department. In fact, the situation escalated to the point where the customer wrote a letter of complaint to the managing director of Tyrrell and Green. I was mortified.

After a lot of digging around, it transpired that, even though I had filled in the form correctly, I hadn't detached the green slip beneath it, the one that should have been sent through to the buying office. I'd left it attached to the red slip, which then sat in the office untouched.

The problem was that no one had ever told me what I was supposed to do. Now, I should probably have been more assiduous in my investigations, especially after this poor customer returned again and again. Certainly, I felt pretty bad about what had happened and I deservedly got a severe telling off. However, what this episode shows is just how important it is to share information with the team. If I had known the correct procedure, none of this would have happened.

There are many reasons why misunderstandings like this occur. Communication processes may simply be extremely poor and/or the induction sloppy. New hires are all-too-frequently expected to somehow learn on the job through some sort of corporate osmoses. Often, though, the omission is deliberate. Those higher up in the organization don't share what they know with their teams. Some managers have the attitude that information is power and they are not going to pass it on to anyone else no matter what. 'We will tell you things on a need-to-know basis. (And, you don't need to know!)'

People don't enjoy being left in the dark. As I know first hand, if you don't have the information, you cannot do your job properly. I was made to look and feel foolish for not getting what should have been a basic process right. Not surprisingly, I was not happy in the aftermath. But there is more to it than that. When managers do not share information, it makes the team feel like they are not important. If they are on the front line, it can make customers feel unimportant too.

I find it interesting that the sectors that are traditionally the most secretive, such as defence, often score the lowest for happiness on the WorkL Index. Clearly, information can't always be widely shared in this sector, but it is telling nevertheless. It is a similar story in sectors like mining and logistics, which often have disparate workforces where it is more difficult to share information. These also have lower happiness scores. One of the big motivations for setting up WorkL was to ensure information is shared more widely with *all* workers. (Obviously within the realms of what is safe and prudent.) I wanted to empower individuals by helping them understand the context for their jobs, whether they were fully trained and what support they believe they are (or aren't) getting. When organizations have knowledge like this, then they can act upon it and make sure everyone is given the full picture. Knowledge and context are really, really important.

At the most fundamental level, when talking about information sharing, what we're saying is, has this person been trained adequately to fulfil the task that they've been given? In my case working in the garden furniture department at Tyrrell and Green, the answer was a resounding 'No!'

There is a second level to this too, and that is, do individual team members have the context to understand *why* things are being done? Throughout my lengthy John Lewis career there would be periods where sales were not as buoyant as forecast. This could be for a range of reasons, from the natural economic cycle, to buyers just getting it wrong and under-ordering products. It's broadly the same in any business, whatever the sector, with a few variables around the reasoning for the slowdown. In our case, the first any of the team would know about a drop in sales would be a series of edicts that would come down from the top of the Partnership saying we needed to address costs.

'Stop recruitment,' the memos to line managers would say. 'Stop any expenses! Don't order anything, not even Sellotape!'

These admonishments would be relayed down the rest of the chain, with varying degrees of embellishment, depending upon the manager. Nobody ever seemed to feel the need to explain why, or the reasoning behind the sudden belt tightening. Hardly surprisingly, individuals on the shop floor were just baffled. When they got together in groups with their colleagues, they'd wonder out loud whether the business was doing a little badly that year, or rapidly going bust in the most exaggerated rumours. The vacuum of information of why simply fuelled the conspiracy theorists and malcontents. What a difference to morale and confidence it would have made if somebody had just said something along the lines of, 'Look, we forecast sales at 3 per cent and they are coming in at 1 per cent, so as a consequence we need to find some cost savings in the short term. Can you all help us think about how we can do that?' When people are informed, they can contribute. They can make suggestions on cost savings in their department, through strategies only they can see because they are at the coal face. Or, they can simply make sure that day-to-day costs are carefully monitored.

Early on in my time at Waitrose I experienced a similar situation, except the messaging around costs was often so contradictory it was even more confusing. The big issue we faced there was food wastage. One month the team on the shop floor was told wastage didn't matter, just make sure the shelves were stocked and there was full availability to maximize sales. Yet, the next month, the edict from on high was, 'We need to cut back on the availability to save on wastage and reduce costs.' Without access to the true picture behind the changes, staff had no idea what was going on. The issue was resolved by committing across the organization to driving availability as a way to grow market share and accept there was therefore likely to be more waste. We choose to generate goodwill for that extra ordering and availability by giving generous discounts on those items that were overstocked, or giving the excess food to charities, or even to zoos!

The Waitrose and John Lewis experience is not unique. This goes on, to a greater or lesser extent, everywhere, all the time. If workers don't see critical data that impacts their departments, they won't know the full facts and will make decisions based on zero, or incomplete, data, which is never going to end well. The R&D department may cut the spec on a new piece of tech because they mistakenly believe the financial situation is a lot worse than it is. The sales team could be more inclined to agree to significant discounts to shift product out of the door, when what is actually needed is for margins to be held at a steady level.

When employees don't know what is going on it really saps the energy out of any organization and makes people feel excluded and disenfranchised. This is why information sharing is so important. If you know what's happening, you can do something about it and you can start taking personal control.

TOP TIPS FOR HAPPY COMMUNICATION WITH THE TEAM   Ann Francke OBE, Chief Executive, Chartered Management Institute

Most people think good communication is about getting their message out in the way they intended. But true communication isn't about what you *said*. It's about what

---

your audience *heard*. Did the person receive your information and understand it in the way in which you wanted them to? Poor communication is one of the biggest reasons for unhappiness and inefficiency at work – so it's truly worth getting right. This is even more important when you're a manager or a leader. If you can deliver your message clearly and effectively, you will be more efficient and focus on what's important. You'll spend less time clarifying your meaning. Your team will have more time and energy to devote to delivering better outcomes and solutions. And everyone's mental wellbeing will improve, as fewer misunderstandings lead to less frustration.

I'm sure we can all think of examples of being poorly communicated with. Perhaps the message the speaker was trying to get across was unclear from the start, or they hid it behind a lot of jargon. They may have picked an inappropriate time or place for the tone or content of the chat, or perhaps their body language betrayed that they wanted to be somewhere else. In each case, I bet you came away feeling frustrated. And I'm sure that many people were then involved in sorting out the miscommunication, resulting in additional time, effort and frustration for all concerned.

Effective communication requires putting yourself in the shoes of your audience. What preconceptions do they have about you or your message that you may need to address? How familiar are they with your topic? On a more fundamental level, are they non-native English speakers? The answers to these questions will change your approach. Making your communication more complex with long words hidden behind a mystifying structure isn't more strategic or professional; it just makes you harder to understand. Think about technical language, too. It may be appropriate for some audiences, like analysts or shareholders, but to others it will appear as jargon. Avoid it whenever you possibly can.

Think about the context it will be received in. Don't start a chat about firing someone by talking about the weather – this will send mixed messages. Likewise, don't start a meeting with your team the first day back in January by cracking the whip – instead, recognize that colleagues will need a day or two to re-acclimatize to the pace of the office.

Finally, use praise (a lot). Praise where it's due is a great motivational management tool. Be authentic, though: make sure your language is proportionate to the achievement and try to be consistent by giving praise regularly. Aim to give between three to five positive statements for every one negative. People tend to discount positive statements and focus on the negatives, so this ratio helps address that.

Sharing sensitive information

FIGURE 4.1   Another snapshot from the WorkL survey, this one shows the levels of happiness about information sharing, broken down by ethnicity

Ethnicity	Information sharing
Arab	70%
Asian/Asian British	71%
Black/African/Caribbean/Black British	73%
Mixed/Multiple ethnic groups	69%
Other ethnic group	72%
Prefer not to say	66%
White	70%

FIGURE 4.2   Responses to questions on information sharing according to
               disability. Again, the higher the number, the more content the
               respondent

Are you registered as disabled?	Information sharing	
No		71%
Yes		68%

One of the most common retorts to this element in the
workplace happiness mix is that it is not always possible
to be completely open with the entire team, especially for
a publicly quoted company which is not at liberty to freely
share data. If sensitive figures leak, it can cause volatility in
the share price and could possibly contravene strict market
rules. Also, in particularly fast-moving and competitive
industries, it is not always easy to pass information all the
way down the line with any speed, particularly when there
are many stakeholders to satisfy.

I accept that things were a lot easier at John Lewis as an
employee-owned rather than publicly owned business. The
Partnership model is based on the fact it is only ever as
strong as the people within it, and the concept of sharing
both data and ideas up, down and across the organization
is therefore more straightforward. Information is, after all,
the basis of democratic participation.

While Stock Exchange rules are understandably strict,
there are still some things that can be shared, and often a
lot more than is currently. I would recommend to any
board to scope out what information *can* be more widely

disseminated. There is certainly nothing to stop companies sharing at least some specific data among individual business units, which will, in turn, help them monitor their performance. If your response to this is: 'Ah, but what if commercially sensitive information gets shared with competitors?' mine would be that it might, but it is highly unlikely. In my experience, if managers trust their teams, it is rare for them to betray that trust.

I would urge any executives to explore how much information they can share and then put in a process whereby everyone, at all levels, is given access to it. The goal is to give out as much knowledge as possible, to give the *whole team* context for what the organization is trying to achieve.

There are other elements of the Partnership which could easily be translated across to companies with different core structures, all of which encourage communication up and down the organization. I would particularly recommend our Branch Councils and forums, which provided a strong line of communication between employees, council representatives and the Partnership Board. Information and knowledge flowed freely in both directions. Union membership never took off in John Lewis and Waitrose, not because it wasn't allowed, but because there was simply no need – everyone in the business had a voice and a direct link to the board. Taken together, these forums helped everyone understand more about what they were expected to achieve and why it was important to the overall organization.

Knowledge might be power, but it is only powerful when it is shared. When everyone has the information they need to hand, they can help find a better way of doing things, more actively contribute and build a better organization for everyone. And, sometimes, the strongest, most motivational benefit of all is when everyone feels they've been included and their voices heard.

CHAPTER FIVE

Empowerment

There is nothing bad about keeping a tight grip on business. For someone managing finance, for example, it is essential that they are on top of what is flowing in and out of the accounts. Sometimes, though, as I discovered with one particular character I came across, things can go too far the other way.

I met the person in question, a finance director, when I was asked to look into what had gone wrong with a division of a large organization. For reasons the main board couldn't fathom, this section of the firm was going downhill fast, just at a time when the rest of the business was soaring. What was going on?

I was tasked with investigating the issue and I got started by organizing chats with the team across the various parts of the ailing division. Even after spending a short time with them, it became clear to me that certain very basic strategic steps were not being taken. What surprised me even more was that the individuals who should have been responsible for making sure these steps were taken had not done so, even though they very clearly knew what needed to be done.

'Why?' I asked.

It didn't take long to get to the bottom of the issue. The answer came back very clearly from each team member: they were waiting for the finance director to sign off the funds needed for the initiative.

'Did you chase it?' I pushed.

In all cases, the answer was a firm 'yes' and, in many, the answer was followed up by a wearied 'several times'.

The obvious next port of call was the finance director's office. Even a cursory glance around the room revealed the extent of the problem. Almost every surface was neatly stacked with slips of paper, no doubt requesting clearance for the actions the various people had spoken to me about.

As we worked through the usual getting-to-know-you pleasantries, the finance director quickly gave away what was at the root cause of the problem.

'I like to keep a tight grip,' he declared, with a visible sense of pride. 'I make sure that *I* sign off absolutely everything. Nothing slips through without me knowing about it.'

Admirable though his intentions were, the accountant had created a hopeless situation. The business had ground to a halt while he personally inspected each individual strategy. There was not even a system in place to delegate to finance colleagues the ability to give the go-ahead on smaller expenditures. Everything, right down to the purchase of a stapler, had to get this man's say-so.

Aside from the issue that essential tasks were not being carried out by the individuals in the division and therefore dragging the business down, there was a much bigger issue at stake here. By behaving in such an autocratic manner, the finance director had taken away all freedom, power, trust and autonomy from each member of his team. It is not difficult to imagine how dejected they must have felt. Ultimately, they did not even have control over how they performed in the jobs they had been given.

The finance director example is extreme, but we see small instances of this type of behaviour nearly every day in business. One of my own pet hates is trying to secure a refund, only to be told by the shop assistant that they only have the authority to give refunds of, say, up to £10. Inevitably, the manager will be called over and it will emerge they only have authority to authorize refunds of up to £50. Again, it's a hopeless situation when the more rungs you have to go up to get authority, the harder it is to get anything done. It's frustrating for customers like me, but what does it say to individuals, when they are not trusted to make a decision about granting a refund or not? Yet, we see this again and again in lots of different guises, where businesses don't listen to the views of the individuals who work there, or empower them to make decisions.

Empowerment is so important. It's more than about giving team members the freedom to exercise personal responsibility, rather than micromanaging them within an inch of their lives. When people are given some leeway, it shows them that they are respected and trusted to do a job.

Empowerment is a crucial business metric

Empowering the team opens the way for them to associate success with their own decisions, skills and abilities. But there is another very crucial reason for doing this: it ensures the business functions better and increases productivity. When an individual feels empowered, they are more willing to undertake more complex tasks, put forward ideas on better ways to achieve goals and work cooperatively as a team with their colleagues.

We usually find the highest levels of disengagement in hierarchical organizations. This is where the senior team make it understood that it is their preserve to 'think the big thoughts' and make all the decisions. Meanwhile, those who have not reached this exalted status are expected to get on with carefully defined, routine tasks, where any deviation from the usual way of doing things is frowned upon. There is zero encouragement for those below

FIGURE 5.1   The results of this WorkL survey show the 35–44 year age group feel the most empowered

Age	Empowerment	
19–24		72%
25–34		73%
35–44		74%
45–54		73%
55–64		73%

FIGURE 5.2   The WorkL survey shows those who are disabled score less favourably when it comes to feeling empowered

Are you registered as disabled?   **Empowerment**

No	73%
Yes	70%

manager status to give feedback, or offer any alternatives to the status quo. Think, though, how different things could be if the *whole* workforce could be properly mobilized. The more junior staff will already understand the business, not least because they will most likely have more day-to-day contact with customers, end-users and suppliers, and more experience of the systems. Given the opportunity to take the initiative, they could have some very pertinent ideas indeed.

Earlier, we talked about how companies often fail to fully explain why they are demanding belt-tightening exercises. Imagine how different things would be if a business outlined that finances are under strain and asked for ideas on how to save on costs. Those on the ground floor might say:

We have identified a better supplier.

The current shift structure could be streamlined.

We would remain efficient if we cut x cost.

Goods are becoming damaged with the current delivery system, we should install x.

By engaging with the team and trusting them with the information, it is possible to gain some extremely useful insights to improve the situation. These may be some 'big picture' suggestions, or a series of little adjustments which, when added together, will make a noticeable impact. Either way, both options will represent a positive move forward towards tangible improvement. Certainly, the impact will be the polar opposite of the response to vague, yet scary, missives from above demanding cuts. Meanwhile, the team will take pride in being part of the solution, rather than thinking they are somehow felt to be the problem.

Of course, businesses need to think about empowering teams during the good times, too. To do this, there needs to be an environment where *everyone* feels able to freely voice their ideas. When individuals are encouraged to speak up, it encourages them to spot problems, take owner-ship of them and collaborate on finding solutions. It also helps everyone be a team player because when everyone feels like they are heard, they are less likely to feel frus-trated, or engage in petty point scoring or office politics. A genuine commitment to transparency and trust also fosters a sense of openness, where everyone feels comfortable about sharing thoughts and concerns without fearing repercussions.

Taken together, all these elements contribute to the professional development of team members, because the practice of sharing perspectives helps us refine our think-ing and expand our skillsets. This, in turn, helps organiza-tions become more agile because, working as a team, it is possible to quickly spot and adapt to emerging opportuni-ties, leveraging the diverse expertise and insights of the whole team.

But, what if it all goes wrong?

The reason why managers and leaders most fiercely resist empowering their teams is they are fearful about what might go wrong. Like the finance director I talked about at the start of the chapter, they prefer to keep a tight grip on things, even if the belief that it is in the best interests of the company is entirely mistaken.

A lesser, yet no less damaging, example of the issue with the finance director is when senior managers give their teams freedom with one hand, but take it away with another. In other words, they let them get on with the job, but repeatedly check in to make sure it is going exactly as it should. Earlier, I spoke about the empty gondola end and the conversation I'd had with the manager. It would have been even more destructive to morale if that manager had subsequently popped back every 10 minutes to look over the shop assistant's shoulder as he filled the shelves. The lad would see that, in reality, he hadn't really been given responsibility for this important fixture and was not properly trusted.

It is worth pointing out here that one of the biggest concerns cited by Gen Z is a lack of career guidance. All they hear is 'You can't sign that off', 'You can't make a decision' (and 'Oh, by the way, we're probably not going to see you in the office for the next few months because we're following a hybrid model'). If businesses want to attract new talent and empower the next generation, they are going to need to loosen their grip and give their teams some freedom.

None of this means that mistakes should just be allowed to happen. There needs to be practical frameworks in place, to manage the relationship between managers and the team. When things do go wrong, there has to be a conversation. Again, though, it needs to be within the realms of trusting the team member and helping them learn through coaching and development, so they can make the best decisions. A manager could say something along the lines of: 'I'm really pleased that you took the initiative to do x, but could you just talk me through your thought process?' Or, 'How might you do it differently next time?'

Then, rather than rushing to judgement, the manager should use active listening skills to hear the answer and show their colleague that they have understood the rationale, before giving them the tools to do it right the next time. A possible response might be something like: 'Okay, I can see why you did that. If it were me, I might do it slightly differently. Here's how....'

The approach here, which is the way to properly empower the team, is to give them the freedom to do their jobs. If it goes wrong, the outcome is rarely that bad or completely irrecoverable, so don't worry. When teams talk about why it went wrong, everyone gains more confidence to use their own judgement.

Getting anything wrong is probably the greatest way to learn lessons. If I think about my business life, I've learned much more from what I've done wrong. Yes, it's painful, but knowing why stops you from doing it again. Feeling as though you're in an environment where people give you the freedom to make a mistake is invaluable. You can learn from the mistakes and move on, all the while growing and becoming more resilient.

CHAPTER SIX

Wellbeing

It's a familiar refrain from the older generation: the younger one needs to be more resilient. If you're really unlucky, this statement might be accompanied by the somewhat toe-curling addition of 'In my day, we didn't expect to be thanked for doing our job.' Or that old classic, 'We'd drag ourselves into the office, come rain or shine, and didn't shirk, even if we were under the weather.'

Gen Z seems to have come under particularly sustained criticism. Entrepreneur and broadcaster Steven Bartlett didn't mince his words when he said that this generation was 'the least resilient generation I have ever seen'.[1] Reactions to his comments were divided. To many older citizens, Bartlett was spot on. They agreed that Gen Z were too sensitive, too easily offended and unable to step up to deal with the challenges and setbacks of daily life. Not so, said those in the opposite camp – have you seen the challenges they have to put up with? Not only do they live in a digital world where they are constantly being judged far and wide, their introduction into the working world has been dismal. Previous generations didn't have to deal with a mountain of student debt, lengthy unpaid internships, zero hours contracts and an expectation that working from 9 to 5, with an hour for lunch, is more of a guideline. That's before you get to the interruption of the pandemic where 'training' became an exercise in listening in to grids of senior staff holding meetings online.

I am going to call it. Gen Z is right and all the other generations are wrong. A lot of the stuff we *all* put up with in the workplace is not acceptable behaviour. It's all very well to point the finger at young people and say they're a bunch of lightweights, but the truth is we should expect to be treated well. It is not 'woke' (or whatever other term of derision is currently in vogue) to show respect and be inclusive. Nor should we just accept the fact that employee stress is at an all-time high, where 41 per cent of workers say they experience it for much of their working day.[2] People old and young feel dispossessed and that they have little control over their working life. That's the foundation for so many of the health and welfare problems we see.

My interest in wellbeing is another legacy from John Lewis. The founder understood the importance of providing health services long before the NHS was established. In a letter to his wife in 1929 he wrote, 'health should come first, income should come next and happiness last of all'. Without the first two, one could never expect to have the third on this list. He was ahead of his time in recognizing that wellbeing is an essential aspect of employee happiness.

To look after the health of his workforce who, let's not forget, worked on their feet all day in demanding jobs, John Lewis employed GPs, physiotherapists and chiropodists in the workplace. He also set up a committee to help any Partners who might be experiencing money issues, offering financial planning and interest-free loans. The motivation behind this was to reduce the stress that people inevitably feel when they have money woes. Partners, as the employees are known, were also encouraged to unwind out of work and given access to a range of societies where they could socialize together, as well as yachts and golf courses for the more active and adventurous. The Partnership also invested in five country homes and holiday centres which were offered to individual Partners and their families at heavily subsidized rates. Anyone who completed a quarter of a century of service was offered a six month paid sabbatical to refresh themselves and try new things. There was also a generous pension scheme, which ensured Partners would retire with dignity. I still find it amazing that this is the exception rather than the norm. Who wouldn't want to make sure that one's best assets – the team – are well looked after?

Creating an environment focused on wellbeing

Ideally, employee wellbeing will some day soon become formalized as a way to do business, rather than a much reduced, optional extra, where managers try to say a few

FIGURE 6.1   The 19–24 age group score lowest when it comes to happiness about wellbeing

Age	Wellbeing	
19–24		67%
25–34		68%
35–44		70%
45–54		69%
55–64		70%

FIGURE 6.2   LGBTQ+ respondents also feel less happy about their wellbeing at work

What is your sexual orientation?	Wellbeing	
Heterosexual/straight		69%
LGBTQ+		64%

nice words now and again. The goal here is to move away from a responsive mindset where firms only react when issues such as workplace stress arise, and instead plan ahead by using holistic, preventative strategies.

Is it worth putting in the time and effort? One hundred per cent. None of the elements discussed in this book are possible without positive employee engagement. This means employers need to create the right environment where everyone can feel relaxed, comfortable and healthy.

The ideal wellbeing strategy should cover three areas: emotional, physical and financial. The first, emotional, is most likely the one most employers think about when focusing on employee wellbeing. In fact, the bulk of workplace health and wellbeing activity focuses on mental health, which is the main cause of long-term absence, with just over two-thirds (68 per cent) of firms actively promoting good mental wellbeing.[3] It could be, however, that employers think they are doing a better job than they are. Less than two-fifths (38 per cent) of employees believe that managers are confident enough to have sensitive discussions. I find this quite surprising. It's the easiest thing in the world for line managers to say, 'Are you OK?' Checking in with teams like this costs nothing, too. Or, if an individual arrives looking clearly under the weather, tell them to go home, rest and recover; and if someone shares that they are worried about a sick relative, cut them a little slack so they can take them for their treatment. When managers take a genuine interest in people's mental wellbeing it will get noticed. It promotes a feeling of control and autonomy among individuals, because individuals feel they are being listened to and properly supported.

When it comes to physical wellbeing, this is quite a broad category which, as well as encouraging safe working practices, can include exercise and lifestyle choices, such as eating well and living a balanced life. Employers can promote healthy eating by providing nutritious snacks in break rooms, or by arranging for weekly fruit deliveries. Just small initiatives such as encouraging individuals to get up from their desks and take a walk in the fresh air can raise the mood. This can be extended to staff activities or team lunches that get everyone involved. Don't overlook the physical environment either, because it has a huge impact on the people who spend all their daylight hours in one place. A little thought around the design and set-up of a workspace and furniture can prevent a multitude of long-term health issues. Think, too, of any team members who are mainly home-based and give them advice on improving their working environment and provide them with the tools they need to do this.

Perhaps the most neglected health and wellbeing area of all is financial. Many employers believe it is enough to provide a salary and, perhaps, the occasional bonus. That's all good (although I would refer you back to Chapter 3 on rewards and *recognition*), but there is also a real need to assist employees with their financial circumstances and educate them about running their personal finances, and ever more so at a time when there is a cost of living crisis. As most people know, the majority of schools are woeful at teaching children even the very basics about money. Too many adults have no grasp of how to budget, or avoid getting into debt, or how to plan for the future and make sure they understand their pension entitlement. Getting into financial difficulties can have a truly adverse impact on our emotional state. There is a real role to be played here by employers to help their teams find peace of mind by making the most of their finances. It also adds meaning and purpose to the cultural mix.

If an organization is spread across many sites, it may pay to make each individual site responsible for its own wellbeing programme by appointing wellbeing champions. Additional help could be provided through regular workshops to help people on the team to build skills and focus on their energy levels and resilience.

While initiatives in the categories of emotional, physical and financial wellbeing, are led from the top, it is crucial that everyone is helped to see they play a role through the way they behave. It is very easy for one individual to undo much of the good work an organization has put into team wellbeing initiatives. Managers who continually vocalize panic about deadlines, for example, pass on their stress to the team and erode motivation and wellbeing. Success and peace of mind are achieved by giving employees a sense of control and the knowledge that what they do matters.

DEALING WITH ANXIETY IN THE WORKPLACE   Luke Fletcher, Associate Professor in HRM Strategy and Organization Division, School of Management, University of Bath

Anxiety is a high-arousal, unpleasant emotional state. We often use terms such as feeling tense, nervous, stressed, on edge or jittery to explain how we are feeling when we are anxious. We tend to feel a sense of fear and worry when we are anxious because we perceive a threat to ourselves or those around us (a threat that could be physically and/or psychologically harmful). Anxiety puts us into a state of high alert and we become hypersensitive to specific changes in the external environment. For example, we may jump when we see a shadow flicker or hear a car horn beeping suddenly in the background. Anxiety is therefore useful when we need to be vigilant about what is going on; however, being in an anxious emotional state for a prolonged period is harmful, both psychologically and physically. When prolonged, it is often linked to poorer mental and physical health and other wellbeing and life issues.

When we think about what happens in the workplace to cause longer term, dysfunctional experiences of anxiety, we may reflect on some of the following:

- **Organizational change**, particularly during periods of significant restructure, redundancy, or redeployment. It can also manifest during 'positive' transformative change projects which may threaten embedded communities/identities and ways of doing things in the organization.

- **Workload and work pressure**, particularly when systems and processes to manage workload are not designed well or are not working appropriately to help people be more efficient and effective in their work.

- **Poor/bad management**; this may manifest as generically poor managerial competency but may also be specifically 'bad', such as inappropriate behaviour, micromanaging, aggressive or volatile moods/behaviour.

- **Difficult relationships with colleagues**, particularly if you must work with these colleagues a lot/regularly or require them to complete certain tasks or processes for you to complete yours.

- **Lack of self-esteem or feeling insecure** about one's self, particularly in relation to meeting specific job/task expectations or certain standards of performance.

The list presented above is not exhaustive; it is just an indication of some likely causes of anxiety at work. What is important to note about these types of causes is that they generally increase the uncertainty of one's future/work situation and they have (or are perceived to have) specific negative repercussions for one's ability to do one's job effectively.

It is also worth noting that some people may generally have higher levels of anxiety than others, due to a range of factors such as genetics/biological differences, childhood experiences, traumatic life events, etc. This doesn't mean that those who are generally more anxious would be termed as having a diagnosed anxiety condition, although those who are particularly highly anxious in most situations may have. What is important to consider, however, is that what works to help reduce or alleviate anxiety for one person may not always work for another. This is because each person will have a different mix of personality traits and life experiences which will not only mean they will have a different 'general' level of anxiety, but also a different 'mindset' or 'experience' around anxiety. Therefore, any interventions or initiatives to help reduce anxiety should have some flexibility to be tailored to each individual and their circumstances.[4]

CHAPTER SEVEN

A sense of pride

Pride is one of the most powerful motivational forces. Who doesn't want to find something that they can say they're good at and that they relish doing? It has a ripple effect, too. When an individual is proud of their performance, it has a positive impact on the people around them, spurring others on to achieve their best. Pride cultivates an energizing culture of accountability, collaboration and respect. People who are proud of their workplace will speak openly and positively about what they do and where they work. It's no coincidence that organizations with high levels of engagement are those that manage to persuade, inform and educate their teams that what they're doing has a real benefit and purpose. Everybody wants a purpose in life. Everybody wants to feel what they do has some value.

Once again, it's an even more important metric today, too. Gen Z are driven by the need to make a difference to the world, and the organization they choose to work for makes a statement about their ideals.

When there is such a recognized positive impact around pride, you'd expect managers would be falling over themselves to ensure their teams are proud of the jobs they do and the organizations they work for. But it doesn't seem to happen. Certainly not in as many organizations as you'd expect.

THE SIGNIFICANCE OF EMPLOYEE PRIDE IN ORGANIZATIONAL SUCCESS   Anne Wilkinson, consultant, WorkL

When people do not feel pride in their organization the consequences can be far-reaching, and can negatively affect the success of an organization in the following ways:

- **Decline in productivity and quality:** A workforce that does not take pride in its output is less likely to go the extra mile to deliver exceptional results, potentially harming the organization's reputation and competitiveness. There is likely to be a lack of commitment to excellence, creating a risk of declining productivity and a decrease in the quality of work produced.

- **Impaired customer relationships:** Customer interactions and trust in the organization may suffer, leading to diminished customer satisfaction, potentially resulting in the loss of loyal clients and damage to the organization's brand reputation.

- **Increased staff turnover rates:** When staff do not feel a sense of fulfilment or satisfaction in their work, they may be more inclined to seek opportunities elsewhere. High turnover rates not only disrupt organizational continuity and the ability to drive the organization forward, but also incur significant recruitment and training costs, negatively impacting the overall success of the organization.

- **Difficulty attracting top talent:** Prospective employees are increasingly considering the cultural fit and reputation of an organization when making career decisions. A lack of pride among current employees can translate into negative perceptions, poor staff survey results and low employer ratings, making it difficult for an organization to attract the talent they need.

- **Diminished morale, motivation and engagement:** Low morale contributes to a lack of motivation and engagement, as employees may feel disconnected from the organization's purpose, values and goals, and be uninspired to contribute their best efforts.

- **Damage to organizational culture:** In the absence of pride, the culture may become characterized by cynicism, apathy and a lack of enthusiasm. A negative organizational culture can further erode employee morale and hinder collaboration, innovation and the overall wellbeing of the workplace. Employees are less likely to be an advocate of the organization and the way they talk about the organization may damage the brand reputation.

Instilling pride in an individual

Pride is closely connected with purpose. We all want to see that what we do every day is worthwhile. Far too many firms make the mistake of focusing on measures that *reduce* a sense of purpose, or indeed any feeling at all that the tasks being undertaken are in any way worthwhile. This scenario is particularly prevalent in those businesses which mostly measure success based on efficiency and

FIGURE 7.1   The 35–44 and 55–64 age groups come out strongest when it comes to saying they are proud of where they work

Age   **Instilling pride**

Age	Instilling pride
19–24	68%
25–34	70%
35–44	73%
45–54	72%
55–64	73%

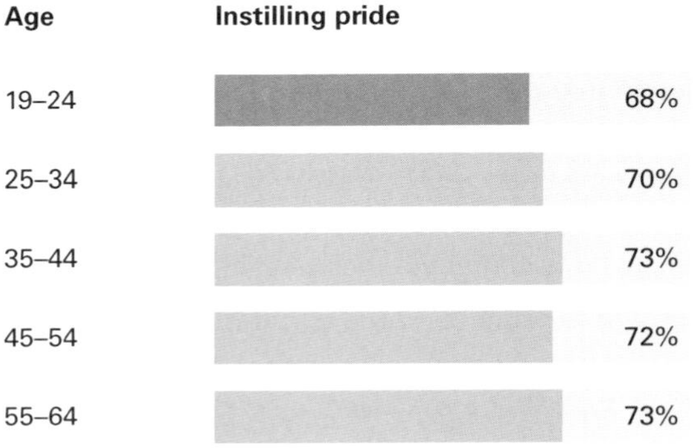

FIGURE 7.2   LGBTQ+ respondents score their employers lower when it comes to feeling proud of where they work

What is your sexual orientation?   **Instilling pride**

What is your sexual orientation?	Instilling pride
Heterosexual/straight	71%
LGBTQ+	66%

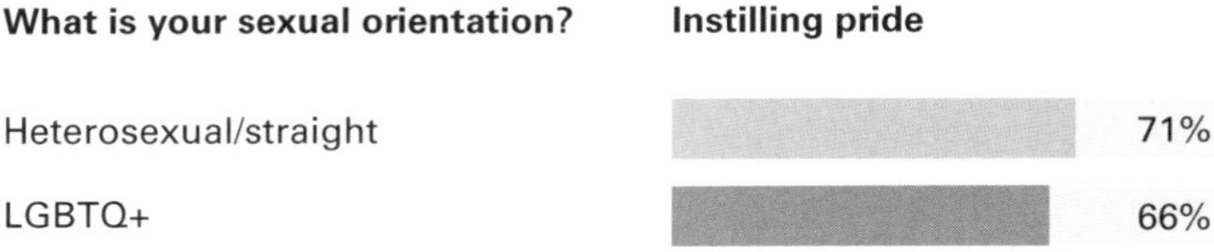

speed of output. Take my old sector as a case in point. Some retailers set firm targets for the number of products a cashier can scan through in a minute, and give lavish praise to cashiers who consistently push customers through at a terrific pace. Attaining this goal naturally encourages intense concentration on behalf of the cashier, which doesn't leave any time for casual interaction with customers. This focus on efficiency isn't just stressful and dehumanizing for the employee, it's also a disaster for a customer-centric business. While the length of queues is an oft-quoted bug bear for shoppers, so is being treated as a mild irritation by employees, and so is needing to pack bags at pace to avoid goods getting tipped onto the floor by the subsequent surge of products racing down the conveyor belt. At Waitrose, we took the focus away from the scanning speed and encouraged cashiers to acknowledge the customer. My reasoning behind this was twofold. Firstly, this obsession with 'efficiency' was not the way to give our Partners purpose. No one wants to be treated like a machine. Secondly, it is probable that, for at least one customer each shift, the cashier would be the only person they speak to that day. We told the cashiers again and again, 'You are the face of Waitrose and therefore the interaction you have with customers is incredibly important.' They were at the front line of whether people had a great shopping trip, or a poor one. It could even have an impact on whether the customer came back or never returned. Cashiers are absolutely fundamental, and that is something they should be proud of.

Aside from the increased engagement from cashiers through giving them this sense of purpose, there was a real benefit to Waitrose, too. The cashiers were on the front line, speaking with customers and, therefore, party to some hugely valuable intelligence. As part of their interactions with the team, managers could ask, 'Harry, what are customers saying to you? What do they like and what don't they like? What couldn't they find? What should we sell?' It was another great way to involve that individual, recognize them and tell them that they are doing a really good job, while at the same time getting some useful business feedback.

Many of the elements discussed so far in this book add to an individual's sense of purpose. It generates pride, for example, when employees feel empowered and are trusted with a high level of autonomy in their roles. When individuals are given choices and the freedom to make decisions and contribute their unique skills to their work, it gives them a sense of ownership and responsibility. Empowered employees are more likely to take pride in their work, viewing it as a reflection of their skills and capabilities.

Leaders who invest in the professional development of their team members are also demonstrating a commitment to the growth and success of each individual. When individuals are given training and opportunities for career enhancement, it not only boosts employee confidence but also instils pride in their evolving expertise and contributions to the organization.

Don't forget the easy wins, either. At the simplest level, the best way to instil pride throughout an organization is to regularly acknowledge and appreciate the efforts of teams. Once again, this can be as straightforward as a note or email saying 'Well done'. It takes very little effort, but is a highly effective strategy for generating and instilling pride. There is also an opportunity to actively recognize individual and team achievements through formal awards. Celebrations create a positive and uplifting environment, reinforcing a sense of pride in the shared successes of the team.

Regular positive reinforcement tells everyone that the organization values the hard work and dedication of its employees, fostering a positive atmosphere of pride.

Promoting pride in an organization

While people want a personal feeling of purpose, pride also stems from what the business as a whole stands for – its ultimate purpose, and the values that are tied around how things are done on a day-to-day basis. Many people, and Gen Z in particular, are looking for jobs where the business's purpose goes well beyond returning a shareholder profit. They want to see a clear commitment to making the world a better place, which makes any organization that achieves this an aspirational place to work. These commitments could fall into the categories of any, or all, of the following goals:

- taking responsibility to support the wellbeing of the environment
- being ethical in all its practices
- supporting the success of suppliers and the communities in which it trades

- encouraging trust between clients and staff
- enabling social mobility through worthwhile, rewarding employment
- offering opportunities to develop

If an organization has a clear sense of purpose, it is crucial that it should communicate it well to everyone on the team. One of the foundational elements for instilling pride in an employing organization is a clear and transparent promotion of its purpose. Business leaders need to articulate a compelling vision that goes beyond profit margins and market share. When employees understand the deeper meaning behind their work and connect with the values of the organization, it creates a sense of purpose that fuels pride.

At the same time as conveying the company-wide purpose, managers should help by giving everyone the context around their personal contributions and how it supports the organization's purpose. In other words, why what they are doing is so important. At Waitrose, there was a Community Matters initiative where shoppers were given a green token at the end of each shop. As they exited the store, they were invited to post the token into one of three boxes, each of which was dedicated to a local charity. The more tokens in each box, the bigger the donation. What made this all the more powerful was that the Partners in each store were entrusted with the task of choosing the local beneficiaries. The scheme, which raised tens of millions for thousands of local charities, made everyone in each store feel good. It was a real morale-booster.

Today, nearly every firm of any size runs a plethora of environmental, social and governance (ESG) initiatives to show they are acting responsibly. There are real opportunities here to boost pride in the business, and this does take some thought. For a start, everyone should feel they have a part to play in these initiatives, whether it is volunteering for a few days a year, or taking part in company-wide fundraisers. There is also an opportunity to really bring corporate values to life and further engage the team by closely tying activities into the skills and professional goals of the team. A large tech firm, for example, might share some of its services and facilities to help train underprivileged youngsters, or older people in IT skills. Members of the team could be assigned to volunteer their services for a few days a month. This adds to that all-important sense of pride and purpose for the IT specialists, who feel like they're doing more than a job – they and their firm are actually making a difference. Meanwhile, for the firm in question, it reinforces their expert credentials in IT.

Think, too, about involving the team more closely in the choice of activities or, better still, allow them to lead a programme of events. A centralized dedicated 'sustainability team' might appear to be the best option to keep everything organized and on track, but other team members will feel disconnected if there is a constant stream of requests to do this or that while they are offered no real involvement in the decision-making process. From a purely practical standpoint, those on the ground floor often know a lot more about where the true wastage is happening and could most likely make some pertinent suggestions if asked. When people feel part of something and that they have contributed to a positive outcome, it instils pride and improves motivation and engagement.

The goal here is to create an environment where people feel engaged and work hard because they want to, not because they have to. Any firm that finds a member of its team saying 'I work for X Company. We do these wonderful things, and I know that I'm an important part of their success' has cracked it. They'll get more from their people and they'll be more successful than their competitors.

CHAPTER EIGHT

Job satisfaction

The concept of job satisfaction is, at its heart, fairly
simple. It boils down to, 'Do I actually love the job that
I do?' Sadly, for a large number of people, the answer
frequently comes back as a resounding 'No!' I've had experience of this myself and it was not a nice place to be.
While I am, as I have shown, a huge advocate for John
Lewis and the Partnership model, there were a few positions I held there that I just didn't enjoy. The reason I
stayed, though, was that I loved the company and the
people there. I took a conscious decision to take the medi-
cine and stick with it, because I was certain I would only
need to do so for a defined period of time, and would then,
most likely, move on into a role I enjoyed. Plus, I saw it as
part of the learning experience. Of course, I was fortunate.

I was on a clearly defined career trajectory. For others, though, they are left with the constant impression that the future is bleak and the only option is to move on.

The financial impact of high staff turnover can be crippling for even large businesses with deep pockets (not that any business can be complacent about losing staff). The average cost to hire a new employee is £3,000, but this figure can rise considerably depending upon the seniority of the position.[1] There can also be a period where colleagues are obliged to fill in the gaps while the recruitment process grinds on, perhaps increasing their own job dissatisfaction. When you add the training bill for each new team member into the mix, the cost rises even further. As the CIPD's Peter Cheese shows in the following section, some industries are more vulnerable than others, meaning the search process is protracted and the task of replacing key members of staff prohibitively high.

What I find fascinating is that many organizations appear to be in denial about the true extent of the impact of high staff turnover. There is certainly a misunderstanding around the difference between staff turnover and staff retention. It is crucial to measure and understand both. *Staff turnover* is the total number of people who leave in a year as a percentage of the total workforce. Thus, if you employ 100 people and 70 leave, this implies a staff turnover of 70 per cent. However, *staff retention* measures the number of employees who were with an organization throughout the year. Therefore, in the example above, if 30 people were with this business throughout the year then staff retention is 30 per cent. That would suggest staff turnover is fairly evenly spread across the business. However, if 90 people out of the 100 were there throughout the year (making the retention rate 90 per cent) but the other 10 roles turned over multiple times in a year, that creates a very different picture. Knowing this level of detail helps organizations to quickly pinpoint problem areas/departments/managers and resolve the issue. This knowledge should very much shape and underpin any recruitment strategy towards the goal of having the lowest possible staff turnover.

SECTORS MOST VULNERABLE TO FLIGHT RISK   Peter Cheese, CEO, CIPD

Recruiting and retaining the people with the skills and experience an organization needs is a critical business challenge and has become harder in recent years. A rapidly shifting job market and changing skills needs, periods of low unemployment in many economies and perceived trends of lower levels of loyalty or more propensity to job hop, are all factors.

In jobs and skill areas where there are significant collective shortages, organizations can face an almost constant challenge of retention. CIPD research shows that three in four organizations experience difficulties attracting candidates, particularly for more senior and high-skilled roles. Public sector employers in particular reported finding it consistently hard to fill vacancies and this challenges their abilities to deliver. But it's not just being able to recruit the talent – it's also important to *hold on* to that talent. Unexpected and unwanted leavers create a hole, a loss of experience and corporate knowledge, and the pressure to find a replacement. The direct cost impacts are also

---

significant. The costs of recruitment, onboarding and training to get up to speed can easily exceed a whole year's salary, and this increases with more senior roles.

According to LinkedIn, in 2023 the most in-demand skills were management, communication, customer service, leadership, sales, etc.[2] These are more general skill areas which will probably always be in demand, but there is a lot of attention on technical, analytical and engineering skills, with the rapid growth in areas like AI and machine learning, cloud computing, cyber security and data analytics. Specialist skills are needed in this era of digital transformation, but also there is a demand for skills that support important shifts, such as the environment and green transition, as the OECD notes in its skills outlook report.[3]

Sectors such as construction, hospitality, driving, cleaning and agriculture all are finding it harder to find and keep their people. Hence the focus on access to migrant skills and talent, but there also has to be attention to the more strategic responses in how to make the jobs and roles more appealing.

Drivers of job satisfaction

There are multiple drivers of job satisfaction, but the foundation is laid before an individual even joins the firm, at the recruitment stage. The applicant must be the right fit for an organization and empathize with its values. Sure, the interview rounds should rightfully focus on their technical skills, but a large part of this process should also be

FIGURE 8.1   Job satisfaction is fairly evenly balanced across the age groups

Age	Job satisfaction
19–24	71%
25–34	71%
35–44	73%
45–54	71%
55–64	71%

FIGURE 8.2   The picture is more nuanced when considered via ethnicity

Ethnicity	Job satisfaction
Arab	72%
Asian/Asian British	73%
Black/African/Caribbean/Black British	74%
Mixed/Multiple ethnic groups	70%
Other ethnic group	74%
Prefer not to say	67%
White	71%

devoted to weighing up the personality behind the CV and whether they'd slot into the team. Does the interviewer think everyone would be happy working alongside the new addition? Years ago, when I ran the John Lewis department store in Cheadle, Manchester, I went one step further than this. Each prospective recruit was asked to spend an hour in the department they hoped to join. Then, once they'd left, Partners were asked what they thought when I posed the question: should this person join the team? Would they be a good addition? I also found a pleasing side effect to this strategy: the existing team felt a sense of responsibility to the person they'd chosen and did their best to help them fit in when they did join.

Once people are installed within an organization, each of the following has an impact on the levels of job satisfaction.

Leadership

One of the greatest influences on whether anyone feels good about their day is their line manager. The quality of this relationship singularly dictates virtually every impression of the firm. All the things we've talked about so far in this book are driven, to a greater or lesser extent, by a line manager's ability to make their reports feel comfortable about their pay, recognizing and valuing their input, looking after their wellbeing, as well as making them feel a sense of pride.

Reputation

A company's reputation will be a big factor in an employee's overall satisfaction. We looked at the power of pride in the last chapter, and it is important that people are excited to tell others where they work. There is another element at play here, too. Job security and stability are powerful drivers. If an organization looks to be on shaky ground, or there is a slew of negative headlines, or there is a revolving door in the boardroom, it will not go unnoticed. Rest assured that those who can will be brushing up their CVs and looking to the exit.

Flexibility

Pay and benefits do, of course, play a part in job satisfaction, but, as outlined in Chapter 3, there are other elements at work here too, linked to ideas of fairness and fair recognition. With cost-of-living increases and more recent pressures on pay, the focus of compensation has also shifted to flexibility. Flexible benefit schemes tailored more closely to the individual needs of employees, towards help with, say, healthcare or childcare, are seen as a positive, as are extending options for more flexible ways of working. The array of working hours options, from part time, to variable hours, to home or hybrid working and other such schemes, has accelerated post-pandemic. As a result, they play an increasingly important variable in attracting people to work in one place or another. (For anyone who is reading this and thinking this is some sort of 'skiver's charter', I will add to this that I genuinely believe that an individual's output should be measured on the basis of *results achieved*, not upon hours worked. A culture of presenteeism doesn't benefit anyone. There is zero merit in people feeling obliged to spend long hours in the office just to be seen.)

Boundaries

Very much connected to the above is making sure boundaries are set so employees don't feel obliged to be on duty 24/7. Thanks to a range of modern communication methods, we can send email, texts and WhatsApps at any time of the day or night. Senior managers might think that it's a great idea to clear their inbox on a Sunday afternoon by firing off a bunch of messages assigning tasks for the following week. They may even assume that it won't get picked up until the next day and therefore that the recipient will be completely fine with that. But what of the person on the receiving end? They may have glanced at their phone while spending a relaxing day with their family. That request will play on their mind, however much they try not to let it. They'll grapple with whether they should respond with a holding message, or get started on the request right away. It's not difficult to imagine how stressful this can be. For this reason, I make it clear there is no need to respond to communications out of hours and I have included a footer on my emails that says; 'I have no expectation that you will answer this email after 6pm and before 8am.' Of course, if they choose to reply, that is fine. But, there is no obligation and no judgement if they don't.

Trust

Never underestimate how important a culture of trust is to an employee and the impact on their job satisfaction. No one likes someone constantly looking over their shoulder to check they are doing something well. If we are awarded jobs on our merits, we should be trusted to get on with it. I am still always amazed at top-heavy businesses that appear to employ extra layers of managers just to check the layer below is doing what they are supposed to do. These superfluous checkers will often have people above them checking their output. Checkers checking the checkers! Madness. While I appreciate that there are some types of business that need more oversight than others (in the financial sector, for example), there are better ways to make sure that the rules are being followed. I also believe that if employees recognize and appreciate a culture of trust, they are far more likely to come forward and act as a whistle-blower to report any suspicious activities.

Career and personal development

The final element to explore here is career and personal development, which is such a crucial contributor to job satisfaction that I have given it a section on its own. Every individual who works in a business, at whatever level, needs to feel like they are being developed. Yet CIPD research has highlighted that as many as a third of employees feel they are unlikely to fulfil their career ambitions within their organization, and that becomes even more pronounced in lower-paid roles.[4] It might seem like a statement of the obvious, but it is no less important for the telling: career development has a huge impact on our liking for the job that we do. I spoke at the beginning of the chapter about the trials of not enjoying a job. Many people fall into jobs they don't particularly enjoy. However, there is a route to help them start to like it and that is to hold out the prospect of development and progression.

Insights from WorkL show the lack of development opportunities is particularly prevalent among employees who are in their forties or fifties. I could speculate that this is all part of the widespread belt-tightening exercises at a time of a tough economic outlook. Perhaps, also, there is a view that these people will be in the same jobs until they retire, so there is no use spending capital on development. This does seem a little short-sighted though, not least because the person in their forties has at least a quarter of a century left in the tank, and perhaps more, with the repeated extensions to the retirement age.

There is another, urgent, reason to refocus on career development. This is something else that is important to Gen Z, which by the early 2030s will make up over one-third of the workforce. And don't forget that, with more flexible working arrangements, this generation is far less likely to be able to learn on the job by listening to and watching colleagues in and around the office. Therefore, the requirement for formal arrangements to be increased is more pressing than ever.

Once again, line managers have a key role to play. At the very simplest level, line managers should be sure to check in with individuals and have regular coaching-style conversations. These should be less 'Do this, this and this' and more 'How can I help you?'

Simple questions can be hugely effective at beginning this type of dialogue and not leaving people feeling they are being told what to do. Managers could ask:

- How was yesterday?
- What could we do better?
- How do you feel we can improve?

These openers show members of the team that they are an integral part of the operation and their views are valued and respected. Another useful technique is to invite individual members of the team to participate in discussions or group workshops. This also has the additional positive of encouraging team members to think more broadly in terms of the organizational objectives.

Ideally, all of this should be matched by a formal programme of training, so people can learn new skills to train them for the next-level position. It will be energizing for them to see that there are clear opportunities for advancement within the organization.

Forward-thinking companies will think beyond job training, too, and endeavour to find out about the personal aspirations of each individual on their teams. If a business pays attention to a person's interests or, even better, provides assistance in helping them realize them, it will contribute greatly to their engagement.

Job satisfaction is built on a feeling of belonging and feeling attached to a job and an organization in general. It's closely tied with work/life balance, because it is inevitable that individuals will weigh up how they feel during the working day and include their conclusions in their calculations of what they need to do to lead a good life. As with all of the elements highlighted in this section, it won't just follow that members of the team will somehow automatically feel satisfied with their lot. Building a rewarding and satisfying relationship takes time and effort on both sides. The goal, though, is that employees feel excited – and happy – about their working day.

PART TWO

Building a happy team

CHAPTER NINE

The vital role of good leadership

It doesn't matter what sport you follow, you will most likely recognize the scenario. A new coach will come in to shake up a failing team and, seemingly overnight, their performance will be transformed. It seems like a miracle. The composition of the team is exactly the same, with the same players in the same positions, but the results are incredible. The difference is, of course, the manager.

The most successful sports coaches manage to get so much more from their respective players. They'll encourage them, nurture them and work with them as individuals. That coach will get them to run for longer, give a bit more and do additional training. They will invest in a different tactical approach and take the time to bring everyone onboard, even if it means adopting an entirely different playing style that might feel unnatural at first. In a remarkably short space of time, they will turn 'average' into 'good' and 'good' into 'brilliant'. They'll get their team to give extra discretionary effort, and then even more effort. On the back of this, they'll build a huge reserve of social capital. The fans will love what the coach has done and they'll love the team because they're all trying harder and reaping the rewards.

The same scenario is true in business. The best managers and leaders encourage more from their employees. It is this that leads them to outperform their competitors.

The role of management in driving a happy workplace is critical. If I were to pinpoint one question in the WorkL survey that almost perfectly correlates to high or low scores, it would be, 'I have a good relationship with my manager.' If an employee marks that question with a definitive 10 out of 10 then, on average, the overall engagement score will be 84 per cent. If, however, the score is a somewhat dismal 0 out of 10, the average engagement score will be 27 per cent. That's quite a marked difference. Great managers deliver the environment that people need to thrive at work, and inspire them to want to come to work and do well.

It is for this reason that the WorkL survey has dug deeper into the relationship with leadership and managers, and includes a 'confidence in management' score on the dashboard that our clients use. The index is developed through ratings for four key statements:

I understand the organization's plan.

I work in a well-run organization.

I do something worthwhile.

I feel proud to work for my organization.

If a manager wants to build happiness within their work-force effectively, the responses to these statements are a good guide as to where to start.

Before we go into how leaders can build a happy team, I'd like to clarify my definitions of leadership. In my view, everybody is a leader to a certain extent, or at least should be. Even those who do not have 'manager' or 'chief' or 'VP' in their job titles have some leadership responsibilities. Since this is the case, they need to accept the responsibility and say when things are going wrong in their area of authority. If, say, someone is in a customer-facing role and sees that a product range isn't selling, or that customers have had a bad reaction to something, they need to speak up. That is a mark of leadership.

There is a difference between management and leader-ship. Let me explain. Management is about effectively using human or financial capital to get something done, or to get it from A to B. Managers are faced with challenges such as: 'We need to find a team to complete this task within four weeks, allocate roles and responsibilities and execute within a budget of £1 million.' Leadership is more concerned with *why* and *how* it's done, and how to make everyone want to give the extra discretionary effort I've been talking about here. Leaders should be constantly asking themselves ques-tions such as: How do I get these people to work together well? How do I give them a sense of common shared purpose? How do I celebrate their efforts when they get the job done on time and on budget? When do I need to give them a push in the right direction? And, if I do, how do I do it? It's all about how to get *the best* from a team, rather than *the delivery* of a team's work. Leaders take ownership of everything and give everyone the right context.

How leaders set the foundations for a happy team

I have been hugely lucky in my career, having worked for and with lots of inspiring leaders in business, charities and government. I have learned something from each of them. I've also always made a point of reflecting on my own performance each evening, and have made it my practice to make diary notes on where I could have done better. Through a combination of all this I have concluded that leaders need to achieve three things to set the foundations for a team to be happy and successful.

A sense of direction

Leaders need to be clear about what it is that their team, department, business unit, region or country are trying to achieve. Are they looking for the organization to double in size, be the most efficient, the best, biggest or quickest? The potential list is endless. Equally, does everyone on the team understand where they are heading?

It sounds really easy, doesn't it? Yet, strangely, so many managers and leaders fall down on *clearly* setting out what they are aiming for and in making sure everyone is onboard.

There are a number of reasons why a clear sense of direction is important. Firstly, in and of itself, when everyone has a precise destination in mind, energy and effort can be coordinated into a unified plan which leads to collaborative working, building trust and respect. When there is a clearly defined goal, it is possible to measure what it is you are trying to achieve. If it can be measured, then performance can be recognized and rewarded. It also allows this performance to be benchmarked against the competition. This creates external 'enemies' which can be used to further strengthen internal bonds and build upon the common cause. The threat of that common enemy pushes performance to even greater heights. Or the enemy can be extinction itself.

When there is no clear direction, each department or division focuses on what they *think* is important or, equally worryingly, nothing in particular. Collaboration within departments and between divisions will be weak and in-fighting is inevitable, sapping the energy of the whole team.

Great leaders set then articulate the direction and then leave their team to get on with the job, letting them build the detail of the plan so they have ownership of it. They don't micro manage; instead, they trust their people to deliver and, when they do, they praise them. If they believe an individual could do something better, they use this as an opportunity to develop them. They treat all employees, whatever their background, with respect, and demand the same in return.

The 'why' is important

Great leaders help everyone on their teams understand *why* what they are doing is important. As we have already established, everyone wants to believe they are making a difference, doing something worthwhile with their life and that it has purpose. For a business strategy to have real impact, the message needs to be reinforced on two levels. Firstly, each employee must know exactly why what they do as an individual is vital to the company's success. Great managers keep their teams informed about all that is happening in their department and in the wider organization, effectively communicating the organization's plan to help everyone feel 'plugged in' with a context for their work. The second level concerns a wider understanding of what role the organization plays in making the world a bit better.

To return to the ubiquitous supermarket cashier, as already indicated, they should be told that their role is vital because they are the face of the company. Each day they serve hundreds of people, and if they didn't do a brilliant job, smiling, chatting, building relationships and being efficient, it could ruin a customer's day. The experience they give that customer will influence whether the customer comes back and shops there again. But there is more than that, too. If the customer votes with their feet and doesn't return, the business wouldn't flourish, and that could adversely impact a large number of people if the shop were to close. Reminding a cashier of this and recognizing their efforts when they have done well is critical.

There is no better example of setting the wider context for making employees feel a sense of purpose than the story of when J F Kennedy, the then US President, visited NASA ahead of the first moon landing. Workers were lined up to meet the President and shake his hand. When the

President was introduced to the janitor, Kennedy asked him, 'What do you do?' Quick as a flash, he replied, 'Put a man on the moon.' Now, that is a commitment to the 'why'.

Take an interest

Lastly, and most importantly, leaders should be interested in their employees. They need to want to know what they are doing, how they are developing and about their well-being. As Theodore Roosevelt eloquently said, 'Nobody cares how much you know, until they know how much you care.'

The mind of a manager is like the core of the Earth. If it were cold, rather than hot, all life on Earth would die. If a manager takes no interest in the work of their team and what they achieve, how can they praise or coach them? Similarly, if the manager isn't interested, why should the workers bother?

Your initial response to this might be that it is obvious. Of course, leaders need to know what is going on and take an interest. I would argue, however, that this is something that frequently slips onto the backburner when there is a lot else happening, as there almost always is in most firms. Taking a continual interest in your team requires sustained energy and commitment. It can't be a one-off, or something you do when it occurs to you that you've not been too engaged elsewhere of late. It has to be part of the weekly schedule of management activities. While at Waitrose, I kept a list of all my key managers written down on a piece of paper. The list included my fellow directors, but also other key appointments in the senior team. In addition to scheduled meetings, I made a point of trying to phone, or meet in person, for a chat with each of them weekly and would tick their names off my list when I had done so. There were about 15 people in total. Achieving this goal each week was not easy with all the other distractions I faced, but I never allowed myself to push it aside *just for that week*. Those interactions were just as important as everything else in my diary.

In addition to my schedule of calls, I would also spend one hour each Saturday evening calling managers in randomly chosen Waitrose shops. It was all fairly informal. I'd get put through to the manager, who I already knew through my regular walkarounds at our various stores, and check in to see how trade had been. Why? Because it showed I cared and that I was interested. I would also always ask them about their team, to check they were interested in the people in their care. I was leading by example to show that they, too, should be checking in with their own team.

I have worked with so many organizations that go through the motions of showing they are interested in the team. They have suggestion boxes, mental first aiders, helplines, all sorts, but still have poor wellbeing scores. Why? Because managers are not genuinely interested in the people that work for them. They are entirely focused on completing the business task at all costs. Meanwhile, they are oblivious to the strain employees are under at work and perhaps at home. They perhaps think that putting the business helpline infrastructure in place mitigates the need for them to ask how people are doing, but it doesn't.

It is just so powerful when a team of people believe you are there to support them achieve the best results and be the best they can be, rather than them being there to support you.

Training is essential

Well-executed training is vital to the entire concept of Happy Economics; nothing should be left to chance. As I have said a number of times, things never 'just happen' in business. There has to be a conscious decision to make it happen. The same goes for leading a happy team. Good leadership and knowing the right thing to do doesn't automatically come with the job title.

I am, as you will have gathered by now, extremely keen on data. It was the motivation behind starting WorkL, because I knew we'd have to prove the case behind Happy Economics to get businesses to buy into this powerful metric. Yet, one of the most extraordinary statistics I have come across in recent years was not via WorkL. It was from the Chartered Management Institute (CMI), where I was President for three years from 2020. The statistic was extraordinary because it was so shocking. The CMI found that *82 per cent* of people in management roles in UK firms have never had any management training.[1] 82 per cent! When I heard this, so much of what I had learned fell into place. People are not happy at work because their managers don't have a clue how to lead teams. They were promoted because they had achieved a technical qualification or been around a long time. But nobody had taught them how to lead a team, to get the best from each individual to drive extra discretionary effort, to create a culture when people thrive and are happy.

Knowing what we know about the relationship between a happy workforce and productivity, it is easy to see why this is so shocking. If you look at the UK's worldwide ranking in terms of productivity, it is one of the worst. Our engagement and happiness scores are among the worst, too. The foundation for this worrying discrepancy is that our leaders and managers are not properly trained. Equally worryingly, no one seems to have made the link between their lack of skills in this respect and the obvious signs of a fed-up team. Yet WorkL stats show that the UK has the lowest confidence in management score, at 73 per cent, against a global average of 75 per cent. Nobody has ever sat down with them and said, how do you manage people? How do you get the best from your team? What do you need to do to one to get your workforce to give more? I am sure this gap between what should happen and what actually does has repercussions all the way down the line and, again, the figures appear to bear this out. There are 9.2 million inactive workers in the UK.[2] That's a staggering 21.9 per cent of people aged 16–64 who are not in paid employment. This represents the highest level of inactive workers in Europe and the G20. Why? Because people don't want to go to work. Why don't they want to go to work? Because it's not a happy place to be. It's not fun. It's not enjoyable. Sure, many jobs are tough, but with careful management, workers will feel valued and engaged. And, that's at the heart of the problem: managers don't know how to manage.

Digging into the issue further, I have pinpointed that it's the appointment system that is at fault. The UK seems to have the highest number of what I call 'accidental managers' than anywhere else I know. An accidental manager is a team member who was performing well at their job, is technically good and appears to understand the business. A manager's position will become vacant and this person is then promoted into a position of management because, well, they seem to know what they are doing. Zero thought is given to any previous leadership experience or skills in this direction. They are put in charge of a team of people, purely because they were an effective lawyer, or journalist, or accountant. In the vast majority of cases, nothing is done to correct this gap in knowledge, or to teach them how to properly engage with their teams, or empower them, or do any of the things we have been talking about here. Worse still, with a dearth of management skills, accidental managers often fall back on what they know best, the technical stuff. They muscle in to inform their reports how to do their jobs better, or even roll up their sleeves and do it themselves on occasion. What they should be doing is sharing their knowledge to help their reports get up to their level. Is it a surprise the people working under their leadership feel pretty fed up and neglected?

It is an oft asked question: are good leaders born or made? My view is that they are made. 100 per cent. Yes, people are born with curious minds and some are naturally just more empathetic. These are good starting points, but they don't make you into a good leader. Anybody can be curious. Anybody can ask questions. Anybody can listen to the answers. However, not everybody then can go away and act upon what they have discovered to get a good result. Not everyone takes the time to sit down and think about why people gave the answers they did. They don't naturally question why it is that some people are happier in this job than others. Even if they do, they may not necessarily know what to do about it, let alone have a clue how to instil a sense of pride, mission and take them on an empowering journey.

Since most companies do not have management train- ing courses, or are not prepared to send their leaders to do an MBA, as so often happens in the US, how do people learn to manage? (The average employee happiness score in the US is 75 per cent versus 69 per cent in the UK.) How do they get the best from their teams? It leaves so many leaders completely ill equipped for the situations they find themselves in. Think, for example, of the situation where a 28-year-old is moved up the corporate ladder and almost overnight finds themselves in a position of leading a group of 50-year-olds who have been at the organization far longer. This is not an unusual scenario. It's quite a big thing, being thrust into a position of trying to inspire people from a different generation, almost twice your age. If you don't know what you are doing and haven't been given any training, how do you get the best from them? If this 28-year-old had even just the basics, they'd know that they needed to talk to the team about themselves, their families and their lives. They should ask their reports what they enjoy about their job and what they don't like. Rather than to just tell somebody what to do, they could ask them how they think they should do it. 'Are you happy with that? Would you like more time?' They could discuss how it might be possible to work towards helping them to do less of the stuff they didn't like and more of the stuff they did. I'm not suggesting any of this is easy, especially in a situation like this. Some people take to leadership more quickly than others. But with no training it is virtually impossible to overcome the barriers.

Not everybody has got the temperament or skillset to make a good manager or leader, but 99 per cent of people can be made better. Even just basic nuances like the language used can be improved, so managers know the right questions to ask and the best way to pose them to inspire the team, rather than leaving them rolling their eyes in exasperation.

One final thought on leadership. If you've set the direction, inspired people about why their role is important to your success, and supported them in the task at hand, then you need to be unrelentingly positive. When others around might doubt, great leaders keep the faith and inspire others to do the same. Great leaders are optimists.

CHAPTER TEN

Recruitment

Creating the right foundations

The humble CV, or résumé, has been around since 1482, when Leonardo Da Vinci apparently invented the idea by sending a letter to the Duke of Milan outlining his skills and experience. The notion of selling your services by documenting previous positions caught on although, by the Industrial Revolution, it had taken on a slightly sinister undertone. As manual jobs were taken over by large-scale machines, people became akin to cogs in those machines. If a 'cog' wore out and needed replacing, the goal was to find a new one that worked in the same way, to keep everything on track. A CV was the shorthand manual to show that the next cog was up to the job. There was added value in any cog which had been in a competitor's machine, so offered the enticing possibility of a little inside information. Fast-forward to the internet age, or I4.0, the fourth industrial revolution, as it is known, and the CV is looking rather tired. Actually, no, it would be more accurate to say the model has become completely redundant.

The abundance of digital services now available has shone a light on just how clumsy the CV really can be. At the touch of a button, applicants can effortlessly apply to hundreds of jobs advertised across a range of websites that collate all the vacancies by position, region and type of business. For any organization advertising for a new member of the team, the end result is a mountain of broadly similar documents, showing similar qualifications and similar interests. How do they match the right person to the job? Just to get to the shortlist stage involves wading through an enormous pile of CVs, which is both laborious and time consuming. It is also inevitable that some real gems might get missed.

If the situation wasn't chaotic and impractical enough, it has recently become worse. Thanks to the rise of AI and platforms like Chat GPT, *anybody* can write a brilliant CV in any style they please. Fancy applying for a technician's job at the Quantum Quirks Lab?

'Write me a CV in the style of Stephen Hawking'

Since CVs are usually unverified, it is a challenge to recognize whether the claims within them are over-egged, exaggerated, or written by someone, or something, else. Hardly surprisingly, it's becoming almost impossible to trust that any CV is a true reflection of the individual whose name is on the top. It certainly won't show essential information, such as whether the candidate is customer orientated, or open to development, or what drives them.

In Chapter 8 we discussed how building and maintaining a happy team begins before an applicant even starts work with an organization. New recruits need to be the right fit within a diverse team which shares some similar values, or a range of complimentary values; and that means so much more than simply having the right technical skills for the job. It's about the personality behind the CV. If you can't get an understanding of this, though, how can you be satisfied they'll slot into the team?

'Ah,' you may say, 'AI can handle that.' Just as AI has come to the fore when creating this proliferation of CVs, so it can take a role in sifting through them, using keywords. Let's ignore for the moment that many smaller organizations don't have access to these sophisticated machine learning tools. The technology itself is vulnerable, too, because keywords don't always tell you all you need to know.

One of my most abiding memories of how this can go awry is from my time at Waitrose, long before we'd heard of AI, or certainly well before it became widely available, but when we were using algorithms to score prospective applicants. I was on one of my usual store visits when the manager made a point of stopping by the fish counter to introduce me to the new recruit working there.

'She has a PhD in marine biology,' the manager said proudly.

The unspoken implication was that this person was perfect for the job because there was nothing she didn't know about fish.

This was a classic example of someone using the system and deciding the candidate was a perfect match because they scored 100 per cent on being interested in fish. They'd fed them through the computer and it had said 'Yes!' Plus, she had a degree, so was well educated. All the boxes had been ticked, and then some.

I didn't burst the manager's bubble and voice my concerns, but I privately predicted that this fish counter Partner would be gone within six months, as soon as something better came along. If you recruit the wrong people, they'll always go. Sure enough, on a later store visit, I discovered that the marine biologist was long gone. She'd secured a research position in Australia and hadn't given a second thought to leaving the Waitrose fish counter. Meanwhile, that store had been saddled with the costs of finding and training her replacement.

The biggest flaw with the CV is that it only tells us part of the story – the qualifications and experience of the candidate. It gives us no clues whatsoever to whether someone is a good fit because it can't tell us what they are like as a person. The inescapable conclusion has to be that the best option is to ditch the old CV we have been using for more than 600 years altogether and replace it with a new system based on radical transparency. This is the only reliable way that everyone can know what they are getting when they apply to an organization and vice versa. I'm not alone in this thought, either. At WorkL, we've worked with a growing number of organizations who have given up on

CVs altogether and, in its place, developed the Cultex alongside them.

Cultex stands for culture, technical and experience. These are the three vital elements used towards finding the right job. Will the candidate fit the culture? Do they have the necessary technical skills and qualifications? How much experience do they have in the role they are applying for? Get any one of these elements wrong and the candidate will fail. Cultex measures all three. If the marine biologist had taken the Cultex, she would have almost certainly scored highly in the technical section, yet poorly in both experience and culture fit. It is not that she wasn't a nice, engaging person, because she was, but her joy for research, nature and the outdoors would clearly show the fit on both sides was well off.

To ensure the right fit, organizations, as well as the candidate, need to take a long, hard look at themselves and understand who they are and what they want. Do they, for instance, want someone highly experienced even though they will cost more, or would they prefer someone junior and less expensive who will need to be trained up? Once this and other requirements are clear, the application process needs to reflect them. This clarity paves the way for honesty on both sides. In Chapter 2 I wrote about the call centre that was painting an overly rosy picture of working conditions and employing anyone to work there just to get bums on seats. It was a disastrous approach and was only corrected when the firm set out the true demands of the job and the type of people who would relish working there.

To find out more about the Cultex you can visit thecultex.com

A question of fit

To find the right candidate for a job, we need to look at it from two perspectives: what's it like for the employee; and what's it like for the employer?

Let's start with the employee.

The goal here is to get rid of the scattergun any-job-will-do approach, where job hunters apply for multiple positions at once. Yes, for the majority of people, a job is a financial necessity and there may very well be a sense of urgency. But getting the *right* job is what is important. Otherwise, like the marine biologist above, they'll be moving on at the first opportunity, which, as well as being a pain point for employers, can be a stressful experience for employees. The answer to getting it right first time is to be more targeted in the search and understand whether there is a high probability that this job in this company will be right for you. This is where the digital world can make a real difference and the Cultex will be a great help too.

So, where to start? Data is central to the WorkL Jobs Marketplace Model. We have a large amount of data on currently over 70,000 organizations. Key among this is details of the demographics around which people would be the best fit with – and happiest in – each particular environment. Extensive surveys of organizations around the world have given us enough detail that we can say definitively that, for example, white women under the age of 35 who work in HR are happiest in this list of named companies. Therefore, anyone looking for a job can use our Jobs Marketplace database and be assured that if they meet that demographic, that is where they would be best suited focusing their applications. We can also pinpoint the organizations where this same category of people is most likely *not* going to enjoy the experience. (I will add that we try to focus on the positive, as a rule, but this option is available for job seekers.) For a small monthly fee, we will notify people about jobs that are the 'best fit' for them, tailored to their background, interests, aspirations and qualifications, where we know people with their demographics are happy. From this point, the applicant can use the Cultex to make sure they fit the criteria for experience and technical/academic skills required as well as for culture for that particular job.

And so to employers. As we know, the issue here is around the quantity and quality of applications being received, and how on earth to filter down the list to find the best candidates to interview. The first thing to say here is: do not rush this stage. Quite often, there's a scenario where someone senior in an organization panics and says, 'We've got 100 vacancies, let's just hire anybody.' That's the worst possible approach. I've seen it happen a number of times in my career, generally in organizations where there's been a historic recruitment problem. But, even then, someone in a position of leadership should say, 'No, we take our time.' Otherwise, the problem will simply endure.

When assessing candidates, there are three elements that need to be right. The first is in terms of personality, their cultural fit, are they going to be happy? Secondly, does their experience meet the requirements for the role? And third, do they have the technical skills or aptitude to do the job well?

Again, the process needs to be data-driven. WorkL uses the Cultex to screen candidates and identify which individuals are most appropriate. To understand their personality, we've designed a range of questions to get in behind the list of qualifications and experience. We want to know, for example, whether they are the type of person who would rather be alone in a room analysing data, or do they like being surrounded by people? What activities *energize* them? The temperament required to work in a law firm is very different from that needed in event management. Therefore, understanding the kind of natural skills an individual might have, what they enjoy doing, what they don't enjoy doing, all goes towards finding the best candidate.

For the second category, skills and experience, we do a lot of work ahead of the process to understand what is required from applicants. While experience and qualifications are important, individual employers need to make a call on the *level* of skills required for the job. There's always a judgement to be made when recruiting between wanting somebody who knows absolutely nothing about the job but is a sponge and can learn it, and somebody who's super experienced and can hit the ground running on day one. Either option is valid, but employers need to be clear on their expectations, and they need to be realistic too. Quite often, particularly at the mid level, we see a massive mismatch here. Organizations say they want to recruit somebody on a salary of £40,000, but they also want them to be an *expert* in their field. That isn't going to happen. Of course, once the successful candidate is engaged on the £40,000 package, it is inevitable that, with this unrealistic expectation, everyone will be hugely disappointed in the performance of the person who got the job. They were anticipating an expert, but didn't get one. Setting out clear expectations and being realistic about what is on offer should shape who is being interviewed and the subsequent view of the successful candidate's performance. If there is a mismatch, it will always be an issue down the line.

The final, important, test is focused on happiness and cultural fit. I often think here of the expression regularly used in customer-facing businesses like retail and hospitality, that it is better to employ kind people than train people to be kind. If you get the right cultural fit from the off, you can be assured that the person is going to be really happy, will fit in and thrive. In this respect, no training will be required.

A really useful exercise to do is to determine ahead of time what characteristics are shared by employees who have been successful in – or fitted in to – the organization in the past. Equally, what are the characteristics shared by people who have not?

I encountered a great example of this right at the beginning of my career, when I joined John Lewis Partnership on the graduate trainee scheme. I had joined from Lancaster University, but in previous years, the Partnership had mainly recruited from Oxford and Cambridge. They'd done a really good job of getting people in from these prestigious universities, too. However, almost all the Oxbridge candidates had left after a year. The reason for this was a great deal to do with the way the graduate trainee scheme was designed. For the first two years of the scheme, recruits were required to do every base level job in the business. We worked on the shop floor, in warehousing, in admin, accounts, everywhere. The idea behind the exceptionally packed timetable was that trainees got to understand the whole business, so they were fully equipped with the right skills when they moved on to become a junior manager and then into their first management role two years after that. The people from Oxbridge did a few months of, let's face it, quite menial jobs and clearly just thought, 'I've come from a cerebral background. I don't want to do this ground-floor-up business.' Fortunately, around about the time I joined, the Partnership management cottoned on to this and changed tactics for its graduate trainee programme.

Organizations can save themselves a great deal of trouble – and slow down staff turnover – by simply looking around and asking themselves, who's happy here? What type of people are flourishing? Once you know that, bring in more people in that mould and they are far more likely to stick around. It is really that simple.

To summarize, all we are trying to do here is to:

- get to the heart of what people like and don't like
- ascertain whether their skills and qualifications match the job requirements
- match their skills and qualifications against what the company wants

If you can do this, then you'll get the best fit candidates.

Even without WorkL data, there are plenty of things employers can do to assess candidates on these three grounds. At its most simple, pick up the phone and speak to prospective candidates. It may sound arduous, but a five-minute screening call is all that is required to find out if they're worth bringing in for a formal interview. Plus, remember what is at stake here. Get it right and this person will stay the course, which will save a lot of time and expense in the long run.

The purpose of this call is to find out about a candidate's personality. The person doing the screening could ask questions like:

'How do you enjoy spending your spare time? Is it meeting friends? Or do you prefer to sit alone reading a book?'

'Do you enjoy meeting deadlines?'

'What gives you the greatest joy?'

The answers to these questions give vital clues to the characteristics that an individual might have. These can then be aligned with the characteristics required for the job they are being recruited for.

When these filtered candidates come in for an interview, consider going beyond the usual interview questions such as 'What are your strengths and weaknesses?' Earlier, I mentioned the test I used at John Lewis in Cheadle, where I sent potential recruits out onto the shop floor to check if they might be a good fit. If you want to create a truly happy team, there is an argument to revive this practice yourself. Send a candidate to spend an hour in the relevant department and then ask the rest of the team whether they think they'll fit. They understand the chemistry and are in the best place to judge.

As you can see, this is quite a systematic approach and may, at least initially, feel like hard work. But, believe me, it is a lot more effective than just doing what the computer has been doing for x number of years, which is ticking boxes but ignoring the question of fit. There is a very contented marine biologist, somewhere in Australia, that would tell you that approach doesn't work.

CHAPTER ELEVEN

A word on culture

CHAMPIONING A CULTURE OF WELLBEING   Geoff McDonald, keynote speaker and business transformation advisor, former global VP HR, Unilever

One of the most limiting resources I see in organizations across sectors and globally is the *energy* of people at work. People are *frazzled*, they can't wait for Friday and are not that enthused for work on a Monday morning.

Energy is probably the most critical enabler of performance. We all know what it is like to work in a team that feels energized – it can move mountains. We also know what it is like to work for a boss who brings energy, versus one that drains every bit of energy out of us. We cannot be energized if we are not healthy physically, emotionally, mentally and feel that sense of purpose and meaning in what we do.

While it is widely accepted that the wellbeing of employees is a critical enabler of performance and therefore a strategic priority, I would question whether all the various resources and programmes on offer to enhance wellbeing are going in the right direction. Organizations tend to do wellbeing *to* their employees. They have made significant investments in making resources available to their people that will enhance their wellbeing, ranging from a selection of apps, to schemes like ride-to-work. The onus is on the individual to go and use these resources to enhance their wellbeing, which hopefully translates into increased productivity and happiness in the workplace. Evidence suggests, however, that the average uptake of these resources is still very low. One study suggested that only around 5 per cent of employees use the resources that a company offers them to enhance their wellbeing. This implies a strong argument against doing wellbeing to *employees* and that instead we should shift the focus to doing wellbeing to the *organization*. As the Dutch inspirational speaker Alexander Den Heijer once said, 'If the flower does not bloom, there is nothing wrong with the flower, it is the environment it lives in.'[1] The same sentiment can be applied to an organization. It is a question of culture.

It is the duty of any organization to proactively address the culture of the workplace to one that will *enhance* the life of everyone who works there. Imagine an employee value proposition that says, 'Come and work for us because we will enhance your life!' Most workplaces today diminish people's lives. What a differentiator the former proposition would be.

One of the most heart-breaking stories I have come across concerned the suicide of two middle managers who worked in the same organization. They were both in their thirties with young families, and had taken their own lives within a short time of one another. The senior management of the firm where they worked were, of course, aghast that this had happened. They couldn't understand it, either. The HR department were quick to point out that they had done all the right things to protect the team, including making sure mental health first aiders were available to all. A little bit of digging, though, revealed a very different story. The tragedy had occurred during a downturn in the sector and the business had been struggling. Under huge commercial pressure, the CEO of the company had gone all out to win new business. If there was a pitch available, he'd put a team on it. The type of business involved meant that it was all-hands-on-deck to fulfil the complicated tender process, with many of the pitches taking up many, many hours. Meanwhile, the CEO ordered that the costings were pared to the bone, to put them ahead of the competition, even though it meant that most of the bids were going out at below market value. When the company won the tenders, this put even more pressure on the already stretched teams, because they had to work flat out to deliver orders and try to cut corners wherever they could, to recoup at least some profit. Needless to say, having taken on so much, both in pitches and new business, the team was having to work through the night to get material ready for the following morning. It became so bad that these two men couldn't cope.

The availability of mental health first aiders would never have stopped the tragic outcome. At the heart of the issue was a leader who put undue pressure on the team and was not sensitive to their time, or what they were having to do. There was no feedback loop system in the business for people to say 'This is too much.' Even if there was, I suspect the CEO just wouldn't have listened to feedback. His attitude was, 'I'm being driven by my commercial pressures.'

I am fairly certain that this business, given the sector it is in, would have proudly displayed a chart in pride of place, boasting of its values and culture. The reality was, however, far from the way it liked to present itself. What happened there was purely and simply down to poor, you could even say tone deaf, leadership.

Leadership and culture go hand in hand. Good leaders create good cultures. Bad leaders create bad cultures. Culture is the sediment of past transactions. The way that any leader dealt with their team yesterday always has a bearing on the culture of their business today. If they treat the team fairly, the employees will think that the culture of the business is good. If they do the opposite and bully, humiliate, not listen to, or disrespect the team, it will erode trust and create a toxic culture. People will see that their bosses don't care about their welfare.

Culture is interchangeable with happiness, too. When you have a good culture, it is a sure sign of a happy workplace. Happiness is driven through a good culture.

Just as with happiness, addressing workplace culture is more important than ever today. We are in the midst of a productivity debate, where many firms complain they are still struggling to get employees back into the office following the pandemic. Many people have tried working at home, or hybrid working, and are fine with it, thank you very much. When I listen to politicians and business groups discussing the need for improvements to infrastructure, or to offer incentives as a way to solve this issue, I often think, 'Better trains or a free coffee won't do it.' At the back of my mind, I keep going back to a conversation I had with a hybrid worker who told me point blank he was never going back, no matter how much his employer implored him.

'It is now completely different from the time I first started working there,' he told me. 'Now, everything has been cut to the bone and it is all about performance and productivity. We don't even have our once-a-year team away-day. We all really liked them, it was good to spend time together and we used to joke around. Now, it's like going back to the "dark satanic mills".'

While we go to work to get a job done, it doesn't have to be unenjoyable. Some jobs are tough, yes, but the senior team can make it bearable, even pleasant. Even at the simplest level, it's not difficult for a manager to say, 'We really appreciate what you do', or 'I really value your input. Thank you so much for what you've done this week. We really appreciate it.' It's a good start and begins to set the foundations for good culture. Ensure there is a good culture and people will be more willing to head back to the office.

Modelling good culture

The key to developing a good culture is to create an environment where people live the things that we've set out in the steps listed in the previous section. This is where the team shares information, looks after each other and creates a sense of pride. When people's views are listened to and they have good relationships with a manager, feel they've been developed and are growing, these are all essential steps to creating a great culture and a happy team.

At its heart, culture is about how we treat each other how we treat our customers. Individual employees care about culture as it applies to them. For clarification (if it is needed), employees don't care if leadership says, 'The culture we're going to develop is to quadruple sales in the next four years.' That's not culture. That's a management target. Ditto, culture is not management saying, 'We want you to do what we tell you to do.' No, culture is based on building a partnership, where there's give-and-take on both sides.

It takes a long time to build a good culture, but it can be destroyed very quickly, too. In every case, it begins from the top and is built on the behaviours laid down by leadership. The impact of this then cascades down the organization. The CEO sets the tone for the C-suite executives. The C-suite set it for their direct reports, who set it for the next level down.

There is no short cut to delivering good culture. There is so much more to creating a positive culture than putting a poster in reception declaring how things 'are done around here'. From the top manager down, every moment of every day, everyone must exhibit the behaviours leadership want to see across the organization and demonstrate through example how important it is to treat each other with respect.

At the centre of it all is where leadership show what they are prepared to tolerate. Does an organization allow swearing in the workplace, for example? Do managers barely seem to register when team members loudly swear, even in front of customers? Has bad language become part of the everyday culture? For most businesses, it is something that managers do not want. However, if this is the case, they need to create a culture where it is widely known and accepted that swearing is not acceptable. Again, this begins at the top. If a manager overhears someone cursing, they need to call it out. They need to make it clear: we don't want that kind of language to be used. If this happens often enough, an environment will be created where the most junior person will feel emboldened to remind even a senior one about this if they hear it. They can say, 'I feel really uncomfortable by what you said', and, because it is ingrained in the culture, there will be no negative repercussions for the junior employee calling it out.

Empowering people to call out behaviour that goes against the accepted culture is essential. While managers are essential to modelling good culture, there will always be good managers and bad managers. A perfect example in the latter category was a senior manager at one firm who, on bonus day, went around to all the secretaries and junior employees and bragged that it was *his* hard work that had created this bonus for them all.

'It's all down to me,' he said, seemingly impervious to the looks he was getting as he did so.

This manager was undermining every one of his colleagues by saying this. It was fairly likely they'd relay the story elsewhere too, thus further eroding the culture. In this case, the bragger's boss had to sit that person down and said, 'Why did you say that?' They had to remind him that it was not the way to create the right kind of atmosphere in the senior team. It's awful for anyone to say they're more important than everybody else. It was a clear sign that the culture in that organization was already in decline, since no one else felt able to call out this behaviour, certainly not any junior colleagues.

The most worrying sign, culture-wise, is when people don't 'see' something like this. They don't see it because they just think it's a perfectly normal way to behave. That is when any organization has a real issue.

Reversing a toxic culture

A toxic culture is easily noticeable in its various forms. There'll be widespread bullying, harassment, micromanagement, lack of transparency and resistance to change. There will be many other small clues besides this, too. When a culture is really toxic, it is impossible to reverse things overnight to restore the workplace into a healthy, productive environment. Nevertheless, I have come across far too many new management teams who walk into an ailing organization, acknowledge there is a toxic culture and declare, 'We're going to have a new culture.' After putting up three jolly posters on the wall they think, 'That's it – sorted.' It is not sorted, though, not even close.

If people have been treated really badly for years and years, a new team can go in and promise them the moon, but nothing is going to change. (Not to mention everybody who has managed that business before them, has said, 'Right, we're going to change the culture.' They've also promised the moon and not delivered.) Changing culture takes time and bravery and the only way to effect real change is when leadership clearly demonstrates to everyone that they really care about them as individuals and that whatever they say the culture is going to be, is delivered. Is the boss prepared to caution or sack the star performer who models inappropriate behaviours?

Culture is changed through tangible demonstrations of what the new culture will be. Say, for example, the new team announces that it is 'employee first'. From that point on, everything will be about listening to the team and putting their needs up front. Let's also say that this firm has a longstanding policy where every team member has to book the dates of their annual four-week holiday entitlement at the beginning of each year. If an unexpected event such as a wedding arises halfway through the year and a team member is not allowed the time off when they request it, what does that say about the employer? The refusal to budge on the rule doesn't seem very 'employee first'. If the employer is inflexible like this, *that* is what the team will remember. This will rapidly be extrapolated into the fact that the firm is not a nice place to work. There is little point saying, 'We're changing' and then behaving exactly as before. It is the same when promised bonuses are not paid. This is even worse when the management's bonus is prioritized over anyone else's. There are so many ways in which the promise of a better culture can quickly be undermined and the feeling that the new lot are no better than the old takes hold.

Like I say, it takes a long time and a multi-step plan to change culture. Once the plan is in place, the management team need to live and breathe the behaviours that they expect to see on a day-to-day basis, consistently. It takes energy and commitment to change a culture.

The best starting point is for managers to acknowledge to the team that there has been a toxic culture in the past and ask about how they want everyone to work together now. What behaviours do they want to see? It is useful to provide specific instances, such as, is it appropriate that managers phone their reports at nine o'clock on a Saturday night when really angry about something and want an answer? Do we want that or do we not? (Answer: not.) Or, are extra hours expected to be worked at the drop of a hat? (Answer: no.) Then, having outlined what is acceptable, managers need to model positive behaviours day after day, after day. This means showing respect, empathy and transparency, and continually holding themselves and others to account for upholding the agreed-upon values.

Clear communication is an essential part of this cultural transformation and not just in the early days. Managers should speak often about the desired outcome, the reasons why change is needed and the steps being taken to achieve an improved culture. Any concerns or questions from the team should be dealt with honestly and respectfully, which shows an ongoing concern and willingness to listen. This process helps to build trust and credibility, essential elements in gaining buy-in from everyone. And where the new behaviours are being positively modelled, managers should call them out and recognize them. This reinforces that the management has noticed and the right behaviours will be rewarded and, at the same time, the inappropriate ones stamped out.

Particular thought needs to be given to remote and hybrid workers, because people who are not often in the office won't experience direct evidence of culture and any changes, on a daily basis. It is so much easier when to enact these changes when everyone is present in the office. There are numerous cultural cues we pick up almost by osmosis. We implicitly understand what makes up the lifeblood of the organization, what it stands for and believes in, as well as what is and isn't acceptable. The only way to make sure remote workers see this too is for firms to work on communications. They have to make sure that anything that is being conveyed to people in the office is somehow disseminated virtually too. Priority should be given to group-based human interaction, even if on a virtual basis. Add five or ten minutes on to the beginning or end of Zoom or Teams meetings for informal chats, or organize an online lunch club. There is so much to be learned about culture through watching other people, talking to them or being part of a community.

Reversing a toxic culture is a long-term process which requires patience, persistence and adaptability. Managers should monitor progress, celebrate every milestone and work towards keeping everyone engaged. Over time, once the momentum is reached, change will happen.

CHAPTER TWELVE

Troubleshooting

QUIET QUITTING AND THE TRUE COST OF EMPLOYEE ATTRITION AND DISENGAGEMENT   Tera Allas, Director of Research and Economics, McKinsey

Flight risk – the risk of losing valuable staff members – remains a critical concern, with avoidable staff attrition dragging down performance in many organizations. The related phenomenon of 'quiet quitting' – when employees stay even though they are disgruntled – also poses a substantial burden for organizational success. It is not just the direct costs of recruitment and training new employees, or the lost output from vacancies, which is problematic; indirect costs such as loss of institutional knowledge, decreased team morale and disrupted customer relationships can be even more damaging.

Recent McKinsey & Company research finds that around 11 per cent of the workforce can be classed as 'disruptors' – those who are actively disengaged and likely to demoralize others.[1] A further 32 per cent are found to be 'mildly disengaged' and doing the bare minimum (Figure 12.1). McKinsey estimates that for a median-sized company in the US S&P 500 index, the costs of employee attrition and disengagement together are a staggering $228 million a year.

At the heart of every organization are its bosses: they not only control resources and choose priorities, but – perhaps more importantly – signal and set the tone for what is valued and what is not.[2] Leaders who engender trust through careful listening encourage openness, honesty, innovation, collaboration and loyalty. Indeed, an individual's relationship with their boss is the single most important driver of their job satisfaction and engagement (Figure 12.2).

The benefits of satisfied staff go well beyond a single organization, contributing to the greater good. Employees who feel heard pose a lower flight risk and are more likely to be engaged and committed to their organization's success. However, the benefits of a listening culture and effective leadership extend well beyond organizational boundaries. As Figure 12.2 shows, job satisfaction is not an isolated phenomenon that only relates to workplaces: job satisfaction is a highly important driver of individuals' overall life satisfaction and happiness. By focusing on employee happiness, leaders can also contribute positively to the broader social fabric: the impacts of a fulfilling work environment spill over into the personal lives of employees, their families and their communities, fostering a healthier, more prosperous society.

Figure 12.1 More than half of developed economy organizations' employees are at risk of leaving, demoralizing others or remaining disengaged

Employee segments as a share of an organization's workforce, 1%

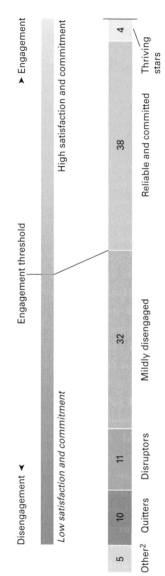

Disengagement ◄   Engagement threshold   High satisfaction and commitment   ► Engagement

Low satisfaction and commitment

5	10	11	32	38	4

Other[2] — Quitters — Disruptors — Mildly disengaged — Reliable and committed — Thriving stars

1. Countries included in the survey were Australia, Canada, Germany, India, Singapore, the United Kingdom and the United States, and the survey ran from November 2022 to January 2023. Figures shown in the graph are estimates based on median size (19,900 employees) and salary ($71,936). Performance and wellbeing data were self-reported and then normalized to reduce the issues with skewed high ratings when looking at the overall sample (n=14,272).

2. Individuals on the borderline of two categories in the statistical analysis.

FIGURE 12.2   The workplace relationship with management is the single most important driver of employees' job satisfaction

Drivers of life satisfaction
% of variation explained by each factor[1]

Drivers of job satisfaction
% of variation explained by each factor

Drivers of satisfaction with interpersonal relationships at work
% of variation explained by each factor

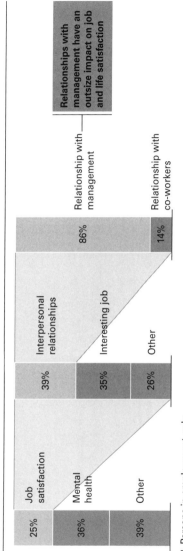

25%   Job satisfaction

39%   Interpersonal relationships

86%   Relationship with management

Relationships with management have an outsize impact on job and life satisfaction

36%   Mental health

35%   Interesting job

14%   Relationship with co-workers

39%   Other

26%   Other

1. Persons in employment only.

There can be nothing more frustrating than bringing a team member into a business, spending time coaching them, training them and getting them up to speed and then, a year later, they walk away. It's even more galling when a firm finds itself having to keep doing that same exercise again and again and again. Plus, as Tera Allas so eloquently shows, the economic impact on an organization can be huge.

Once you understand the full implications of flight risk in terms of recruitment and training costs, alongside the period of reduced productivity while new people are in training, it's not a big leap to pretty quickly get to the point of saying, well, actually, it's better if people don't leave in the first place. Even if not every single member of the team is making an outstanding impact, or is even occasionally getting things wrong, it's much better to keep training and encouraging them than it is just cutting them loose. This is, after all, not a reality TV series, where the boss can glee-fully yell 'You're fired!' That sort of attitude and behaviour is simply not consistent with wanting to build a long-term profitable business. Instead, you need a committed, well-trained and, most of all, happy team which is in it for the long haul.

There is little point managing flight risk after the event. The key to success here is to understand the probability of it happening and then do something to prevent it. For this, organizations need to find out how their teams feel about their jobs. Unfortunately, it is not as easy as asking them straight out whether they are happy in their work or thinking of leaving. While some people will give a clear, open and honest answer, there are many who won't declare their true thoughts. These are the quiet quitters, who say nothing, but work less and less hard until eventually they just leave. They're on the flight path out of the business, but just don't articulate it.

Once again, there needs to be a more measured, scientific approach. What we've been able to do at WorkL is to identify who is likely to leave and when they're likely to leave. There's a flight risk score, showing the percentage of people likely to leave, based on data from more than 70,000 organizations. New starter surveys are useful here, because they shine a light on people's expectations. This is especially pertinent for businesses in sectors such as retail and hospitality, where there is often a huge amount of leavers in the first six months. People start work with the organization and quickly realize that it is not for them and then resign. This is often a clear sign that the organization isn't putting much energy and effort into nurturing and keeping them. Exit surveys are also helpful. When somebody resigns, we ask them, why did you leave this organization? That gives us firm evidence on what was important to them and why they had to leave, and it is insight from these surveys, together with appraisal surveys, that allow us to accurately predict who is going to leave.

As outlined earlier, one of our most telling survey questions is, 'How well do you get on with your manager?' Almost invariably, a shaky relationship with the manager is a clear indication of flight risk. Often, this will be the only negative indicator, but it is a strong enough one to show a clear dissatisfaction and a most likely move towards the exit.

The power of this more scientific approach is that it allows businesses to make interventions earlier. If it is possible to see that people are starting to head towards this quiet quitting flight path, there are decisions to be made. Managers can decide, is this person worth making an effort to save? Do we think that they have the skills we need? If they don't, fine, the process can be accelerated by a conversation about them not really making the grade. If, however, they have potential, they can explore what it is they need to do to encourage them to stay.

Managing bad managers

There are virtually no organizations of any size that have not experienced the fall-out following the actions and missteps of an individual poor manager, or worse still managers. I've certainly seen evidence of this at any job I have ever done. The contrast between good and bad managers was most noticeable at Waitrose, though, because we had multiple individual stores, each under a different manager. Some stores had a much, much higher level of staff turnover, sometimes as much as double the staff turnover of an equivalent shop in a similar area. In each case, it really was all down to the management of those poorly performing stores.

Even without the staff turnover figures, the signs of a poorly performing manager are not hard to miss. The rest of the firm will be doing fine but, in one particular department, there will be the tell-tale increased rates of sickness and lengthy absences. If you pay a visit to this department, there will be further signs. The manager in question will be quick to criticize their reports, or undermine work they've done. Team members may, if asked, admit that this manager takes no interest in them, refuses to share information and is focused on their own progression. Some people will just stick it out, but since they are not happy they won't give it their all. Other people will just go.

I'm always amazed by firms when they know they have a rubbish manager, but don't do anything about it. Perhaps the leadership is too busy, or just don't want to admit it. Or, perhaps, they are not looking in the right place. Most leaders will look at customer satisfaction matrix and at their use of capital matrix, but they won't look at a people matrix. They don't seem to want to know how their team is getting on. It's not seen as part of the equation.

All organizations do need to make sure that rooting out bad managers is at the top of their agenda. This situation cannot be left unattended because, over time, it will cost the firm thousands, if not millions, as the commercial performance suffers. It's also not fair on the individuals that work under these managers and will quickly destroy the culture of the business. The solution is straightforward. Firstly, identify which managers in which departments are getting poor results in their happiness/engagement survey. Secondly, analyse the reasons why. We make this easy at WorkL by identifying the three top areas for improvement and giving practical advice on how to improve. We also have a 'to do' list to share with managers to monitor progress. This list may also include coaching and more formal training. We also offer online courses on how a manager can improve the team's happiness/engagement. If all of this fails to get any improvement then the manager has to be moved on.

None of this is to say every manager has to be the same. In fact, we are all the richer for the fact that we are very different. Some people are extroverts, others introverts. While some are effusive about ideas, others prefer to be silent and to mull it over before they pronounce their thoughts. It is another key leadership role to navigate through this and get the best out of the senior team, regardless of their personality type, so they can get the best out of their direct reports. Get it right and it can improve the outputs for everyone.

I'll share an example from Waitrose. At one time, there were two members of the board who were always at the extreme opposite sides of the debate when it came to how they received new ideas. One was always delighted by the new, eager to explore the options and work out the best way to progress it. The other would start by listing all the ways this initiative could spell disaster. It would have been easy to dismiss the latter character as a bit of a grumpy you-know-what, but I appreciated the broad range of thinking because it meant each strategy was fully stress tested before it was progressed. However, the process did need to be carefully managed.

My approach was to play to their strengths. As soon as any new initiative had been outlined, I would invite my cynical director to be a black hatter and outline all the reasons why he believed it was a terrible idea. The other, optimistic board member was encouraged to outline all the great bits about it. This made it legitimate for the doomsayer to be a doomsayer and the enthusiast to be an enthusiast. No one was in the least bit frustrated. Meanwhile, I had the benefit of a very full, carefully considered dissection of the idea.

Remember, we are all different. A product of our upbringing, education and experiences. No two people will ever hold an identical view. If someone holds a different view to your own, it is best to ask why they have come to the view they have rather than jumping straight in and disagreeing. After you've heard their explanation, you will either be able to change your thinking towards theirs, or better explain why your experience has brought you to a different conclusion.

If a manager's style is grating and team members are starting to leave, don't be too quick to judge. However, do begin the process of having that conversation, to help them lead and engage their teams in the way they deserve to be led.

Dealing with difficult people

For balance, it is useful to deal with the question of difficult people. It is, after all, not just managers who are perceived to be a problem, and people do leave because they simply cannot get along with a particular colleague.

My starting point here is that I genuinely don't think the vast majority of people are awkward just for the sake of it. I believe that there is almost always a credible reason behind why they're behaving in the way that they're behaving.

Listening is the foundation of understanding staff dissatisfaction and clashes between certain groups. The individuals involved are, after all, best placed to voice misgivings about their own area of work and often have some practical, innovative solutions to workplace challenges. To be effective, this process needs to be instigated by managers and happen in multiple settings, on multiple occasions. It might be via one-on-one encounters, team meetings, town hall sessions, informal interactions, or anonymous surveys. It is crucial that the purpose and context of this engagement is made clear, so it serves as a venue not just for voicing concerns but also for proposing solutions.

Managers should work with their reports to explore whether it is the job itself they don't like, or simply elements of the job that rankle. Occasionally, it might emerge that their expectations are unrealistic. In this case, there is a need to put their job in context. There may even need to be a coaching conversation to redirect their efforts. It's all about having that conversation with somebody and putting it all in the right context.

Occasionally, there just won't be an obvious reason for, or solution to, a person's unhappiness in their role, which is demonstrated through their unhelpful or dismissive behaviour towards colleagues. We don't, of course, live in a perfect world. Sometimes, we inherit people who just don't seem very good at their job, or who seem very unhappy about pretty much everything. Once again, the best way to get to the bottom of it, is to begin with a conversation. And if someone is the wrong fit for the job, or the company, then there needs to be an honest conversation. This conversation should begin with a recognition that the person in question has skills, but, through no fault of their own, the fit isn't there. Managers should emphasize that they will do everything they can to help and this includes, if necessary, assisting their move to somewhere where they can flourish. First though, there needs to be a serious discussion. There is zero point second-guessing what the problem might be. You will almost certainly get it wrong.

SPEAKING WITH AND LISTENING TO DIFFICULT PEOPLE: STRATEGIES FOR SUCCESS   Yvette Ankrah MBE

Dealing with difficult people is a common challenge in both personal and professional life. By learning how to navigate challenging interactions, we develop skills for maintaining healthy relationships and personal wellbeing.

We never know what people are going through. We are holistic beings – if issues are happening outside of work, they can have an impact in the workplace. Behaviour is always trying to communicate something. Their behaviour may be a result of other things and may have little to do with you.

An effective strategy to begin with is to ask who you are in this. Being aware of our own state and behaviours is important when dealing with others. Remaining calm and keeping your composure ensures that the situation does not escalate and a solution can be more easily reached. When calm, if someone is being aggressive, we can respond rather than react.

If you are regularly having negative interactions with a person, consider what it is about their behaviour that triggers you. Also, reflect on how you interact. You may have needed to be more open, engaged better, or responded differently in a specific situation. The more we develop our emotional intelligence, the more we can understand ourselves and have empathy for others.

We all view the world through our specific lenses. Therefore, in these situations, start by approaching the person with compassion. What is going on with this person? What is motivating their behaviour? Acknowledge their feelings, even if you don't agree with their actions. Using empathy may help you to connect.

Very often, people want to be heard and, by taking the time to actively listen to them, you may find out what is going on and why they have been difficult. Ask the question: how can we find better ways to work together? You'd be surprised at what you'll find out, not least because others may have not bothered to invest the time with them. When people are deemed 'difficult', they are often avoided and sidelined, which can build their resentment. They lose their voice. Their perspective on issues is then lost, even though they may have knowledge or awareness that is needed.

Remember, you are colleagues, not combatants! Not every disagreement requires a full-blown confrontation. How important is the issue to you? Is it worth the energy to engage in a dispute? Sometimes, letting go of an issue can contribute to a more harmonious working relationship.

PART THREE

Maintaining a happy organization

CHAPTER THIRTEEN

Corporate happiness plan

All businesses make plans, at least the most successful ones anyhow. They make plans for strategy, finance, operations, risk, quality control, tech implementation and much more. Without a detailed plan it is impossible to guide their actions, effectively allocate resources, anticipate challenges or identify opportunities. Given what we've been discussing here, it's a big mystery to me why the vast majority of organizations wouldn't even consider a corporate happiness plan.

Creating a happy organization doesn't just happen. As I have shown many times here, there are too many vulnerable points, not least the vast numbers of accidental managers who can easily scupper the best of intentions. In this final chapter, I'd like to propose that a corporate happiness plan takes its rightful place alongside all the other strategic plans that underpin businesses. This plan should be built around an understanding about what it is that drives a good culture and happiness at work. This plan will tackle all areas, from staff development, to diversity and inclusion, to wellbeing improvement and rewards and recognition, to ensuring the whole team has a sense of pride and satisfaction in their career.

The corporate happiness plan must start with an assessment of the situation as it is today. In other words: ask the team what they think. Set up a survey to identify the pain points, areas where employees are unhappy, or experiencing challenges. This exercise will almost certainly show up a number of areas of dissatisfaction, or levels of concern, about everything from workload, to work/life balance, to communication, recognition, career development or culture. All the things we've been talking about here, in fact.

The good news is, even by asking, a big step forward has been taken. Involving the team in this assessment process encourages their engagement. It shows that the organization is listening. Of course, though, this is just the start. If a particular area emerges as weak, remedial action is required. In the following sections I have broken down possible actions for each of the six elements outlined here. If, for example, your employee survey shows that there is a big issue with information sharing in your organization, that section will outline a number of possible remedies to resolve the issue and signal to the team that things are changing.

It should go without saying that the initial employee survey is not a one-off. The team needs to be deeply involved with the corporate happiness plan all the way through its implementation. When, say, the management team begins to tackle the issue with information sharing, the process should start with proper discussions between managers and team members. This can be via individual one-to-one meetings, or via a questionnaire. Managers should begin by asking team members to share their thoughts on what information they feel they don't have and why it is important to them. The same goes for each of the six elements where issues have been identified. Managers need to take the time to question team members on their views on fair pay for their job, thoughts on wellbeing and so on. Active listening is key here. In one-to-one meetings, managers should let people talk uninterrupted and remain calm and open to their views, even if what is being said is not what they want to hear. Once team members have said their piece, clarifying questions can be asked to build on the understanding of what has been discussed. The meetings should end with a manager's summary of the key points to show they've understood.

Often, we get situations where managers insist something is happening, even though their team says the opposite. The survey will reveal concerns over being kept in the dark about x, y or z and a manager will retort, 'But we've openly published a document on that!' It is only when pressed that it will emerge that this document is in the darkest corners of the corporate website and impossible to find by all but the most tenacious investigators. This is why these live discussions are so important. Listen carefully and these issues can be easily fixed.

Before we get into the detail, to reiterate, this is not a one-off exercise. Managers should be sure to discuss with the team any actions that are taken in response to this feedback, although hopefully they will notice some of the steps taken to improve the happiness of the organization. There should also be a repeat of the corporate happiness assessment at the end of each year. Following the initial survey, there is now a baseline measurement. This is great to track improvements in happiness levels over time and really useful to spot problem areas where things have gone off the boil.

And so to the plan. In the following sections, there are a number of suggested actions. They are built around some of the questions that WorkL uses in its surveys, but, as you will see, the issues highlighted are common to most organizations. Take the remedies you believe are most appropriate according to any issues identified in your own business and use them as the basis to build your own bespoke corporate happiness plan. I have also included some suggested phrases, which managers might like to use to begin the conversation with the team.

Reward and recognition

Pay often comes up as a bugbear among employees, but when you get into the detail, there is almost always more to it. If you're building a plan and you think that recognition is an issue for the team, then questions need to be asked about how you formally and informally improve on the situation. How do you make your people feel that you're recognizing their performance and appreciate them?

Concerns over fair pay

- **Provide transparent pay structures and relevant information, so everyone on the team can judge whether their pay is fair**

  Eliminating secrecy about pay structures creates a healthy work environment and builds trust between the team and management. This is not a one-off exercise. Managers should regularly share details on any changes to pay regulations, industry standards and local pay rates. Highlight changes to the national minimum wage and inflation, with an explanation of how it might impact pay.

- **Ensure managers are confident and effective in managing pay**

  If there is a pay policy in place, ensure everyone is confident about explaining it and applying it for the people in their team.

- **Be open to discussing any pay concerns**

  If a pay range exists, managers should be able to tell each employee where they sit on that range and why. They should also clearly lay out how each individual can move along the scale and support them in any personal development plan that will help them effect this.

SUGGESTED PHRASES

'Let's run through your responsibilities and tasks and compare them to your job description.'

'It would be great if we could have a discussion about your pay concerns, so we can create a development plan that you can bring to your next pay review to make sure your contribution is reflected in your pay.'

Concerns over hours worked

- **Communicate with the team about working hours**
  Once again, this should begin with a discussion to clarify what individuals feel about their working hours. Active listening is key, followed by a summary to show that the manager understands what's been said.
- **Implementing a culture that encourages work/life balance**
  Managers should show they support a better work/life balance among team members by:
  - allowing flexible working schedules
  - ensuring, where possible, that effective hybrid working arrangements are in place
  - working with individuals to review policies and develop ways of working to meet their changing needs
  - ensuring that wellbeing and happiness are at the centre of how the team operates
- **Monitoring workload and the distribution of working hours**
  Managers should be alert to the negative impact on individuals through the allocation of working hours. If additional work is required, they should endeavour to provide a reasonable amount of notice and support so

people can effectively manage their lives. This is particularly pertinent to team members on zero hours contracts.

- **Communicate about rotas**

  If rotas are used, managers should consult with the team to see how well existing rotas are working and be open to introducing a more efficient system that is better for work/life balance, while also enabling the business to succeed.

- **Respect and protect the personal time of individual team members**

  Clear standards and expectations should be set about protected time. This might include laying out whether it is acceptable to send emails in the evening or over the weekend. Managers should also act as role models, taking breaks and their full holiday entitlement.

- **Help team members to manage their time effectively**

  Managers should become rigorous in establishing clear priorities and setting realistic targets. Initiatives can include:

  - avoiding ambiguous job briefs and arbitrary deadlines
  - encouraging individuals to speak up if they have concerns about workloads
  - intervening and offering support if an individual is struggling with their workload
  - if the workload always seems too much, there is a strong argument for conducting a thorough time-and-process study to uncover in efficiencies, or determine whether further resources are required

- **New roles and additional hours should be made available to all, where possible**
  Managers should be transparent and fair if new roles or additional hours become available, so that everyone has an equal chance to apply.

SUGGESTED PHRASES

'As a team, do you think we have a good work/life balance?'

'How can I (and the business) support you to spend your working hours more productively?'

'Can you all write down the hours that work best for you, then the hours you can do but would prefer not, then lastly the hours that are absolutely not possible? Please be realistic, since we want this to work for as many people as possible.'

Concerns over lack of recognition

- **Create a culture focused on recognizing good work**
  Managers should regularly tell individuals they are appreciated for their efforts. Also, they should encourage everyone to recognize one another, to create a high degree of social wellbeing, which is a vital component to overall wellbeing.
- **Managers should meet regularly with teams, either virtually or in person, to talk about performance**
  The goal here is to talk about successes and be positive and encouraging, at the same time as providing regular

coaching and feedback. This is a dynamic and supportive way to help individuals feel they are learning, rather than being criticized.

- **Make time in the schedule to deliberately notice good work**

    It's good practice to set aside time to notice high-quality work, problem solving, extra effort and teamwork, and to thank people. Public acknowledgement is a great tool to inspire and motivate, while positive reinforcement is an effective way of teaching and encouraging a repeat of positive behaviours. Failures should be discussed in private, with the emphasis on finding solutions and learning.

- **Be creative with recognition**

    A simple thank you is great, but managers can mix it up with initiatives like taking a team member for lunch, or awarding them an extra day's holiday. The Chairperson or CEO should take a part in recognizing really outstanding work.

SUGGESTED PHRASES

'I acknowledge that you don't always feel recognized. What forms of recognition would you benefit from?'

'How could I better recognize you for the work you do?'

'I would like to have a five-minute chat with each member of the team, every month, to talk about the great work you've done that month.'

Information sharing

The goal here is for managers to listen to the views and ideas of their team and, where extra training or development is required, arrange it.

Concerns that team members don't have enough information

If there are concerns that team members don't have enough information (and training) to do their job well:

- **Ensure the necessary information is communicated and easily accessible**
  Team members should also be encouraged to keep themselves up to date.
- **Managers should take full responsibility for ensuring their teams have easy access to training and the information they require**
  This also includes identifying any missing materials, or if any existing materials are not up to date. Managers can work with relevant departments to develop appropriate resources such as training programmes. They can then schedule time to provide these resources to the team and make sure everyone is given adequate time to complete their training.
- **The goal is to create a culture where learning on the job is part of everyday routine**
  Promoting the acquisition of skills among the team encourages them to learn from each other and solve problems together. This, in turn, creates a working environment where people are willing to learn and teach others skills.

'What are the areas where you think you would benefit from some additional support?'

'Have you heard about the x training course that is coming up? Would you be interested in taking part to help advance your career?'

'Do you know how to access x? I believe it has a lot of the information you are asking for.'

Concerns that information is not regularly and openly shared

- **Managers should ensure they are well informed and encourage the team to do the same**
  Teams need to know the context of what is happening in an organization and why decisions are being taken. It helps them make sense of how it is being run. Managers should prioritize sharing information and point out items of particular interest or relevance.

- **Think about the delivery**
  It's a manager's responsibility to confidently share the facts in a simple and factual manner, giving examples of how what is being communicated impacts each individual and their work. They should also make sure that anyone who misses a briefing is brought up to speed at a later date. Any manager who does not feel confident or skilled in presenting and sharing information should access training.

- **Remember remote and hybrid workers**
  Those working outside of the main office often feel out of the loop. Managers should make an extra effort to communicate with remote workers using video conferencing and online tools such as Slack. Team chat apps can be used to share files and edit them in real time, so all team members can easily collaborate.

> **SUGGESTED PHRASES**
>
> 'I can share more information with you in the following ways. Is there anything else you think you need?'
>
> 'Let me show you how you can access x, so you can feel more informed.'

Concerns that views go unheard

- **Managers should always actively listen to their team**
  It is crucial to set the tone for non-judgemental, inclusive and respectful behaviour and managers can do this by focusing on what is being said and ignoring distractions. Techniques such as quiet and loud listening can be useful. Quiet listening is where one party is silent and gives others room to talk. Loud listening is where one side puts out an opinion and encourages others to challenge them.
- **Diversity is key**
  It is important to create a work environment that not only feels inclusive, but which also provides everyone on the team with those they can relate to and look up to.

Managers should acknowledge the differences throughout their teams and ensure every team member is heard and able to be themselves. When everyone can contribute, it brings a variety of perspectives, which always leads to the best ideas and outcomes.

- **Encourage input from everyone**
  To set the scene, gather thoughts and views:
  - Facilitate idea-generating sessions that are fun. Managers should be encouraging and manage the process to keep it on track, focused on ideas and solutions, as well as making sure everyone listens to one another.
  - Flipcharts and whiteboards are useful for brainstorming in person and online.
  - Make it comfortable for people to disagree or offer alternative solutions.
  - Avoid making decisions just because the debate has gone on for too long, or seems painful.

- **Create a safe space to nurture new ideas**
  Everyone should be encouraged to regularly submit suggestions and raise concerns. It is helpful to introduce an easily accessible, simple system to generate ideas or voice complaints. Managers should make sure that any issues raised are quickly addressed.

- **Different personalities have different ways of communicating**
  Build a culture around team discussions where *everyone's* voice is heard, not just the loud ones. This means ensuring meetings are inclusive, so every participant is given a chance to speak, and may entail working one's way around the group. Online and virtual attendees should not be forgotten either, and should be told to

raise their hands and leave comments when they want to speak.

- **Encourage a culture where team members feel happy about coming forward with their views, ideas and problems**

  Empower everyone to point out what needs improvement. A big part of this is actually making changes when they do. Managers should make themselves available, which sends the message that the team can approach them with anything, including their career plan and personal development. In one-on-one meetings people should always be asked if there is anything further they'd like to raise and discuss.

SUGGESTED PHRASES

'What can we do to support you to feel more heard?'

'Can you share some examples of where you haven't felt heard or listened to?

'Let's have a one-to-one conversation, so we can work on this and make sure you don't feel like this again.'

Concerns from individuals that they don't understand the organization's plan

- **Communicate details of the plan**

  Managers should organize a briefing session and encourage all team members to attend. Full context should be provided so everyone understands the decisions that have been made. Include a Q&A session to go into the detail.

- **Provide the team with regular updates**
  The above should not be a one off.

SUGGESTED PHRASES

'I would be happy to sit down with you and explain the organization's future plan, as well as give you some reasons behind it.'

Empowerment

Staff are more likely to be happy at work if they feel trusted and appreciated, have a decent level of autonomy and feel they fit in with an organization. But we are all individuals and are motivated by different things. To understand why engagement levels are low, managers need to get into the detail.

Concerns over freedom to make decisions

- **Make decision making collaborative**
  Brainstorming sessions are a good way to get the process started. After stating a goal, managers can ask for input on how best to get there. They may already have a firm vision for how to execute it, but others on the team may well have ideas on better ways to complete the task. To get the best results, managers should be encouraging and show they are open to new ideas.
- **Invest in the team**
  When managers properly get to know and understand individual team members, it helps them lead

more effectively. Giving them a chance to shine empowers people to use their strengths and judgement. Invest in training and development to help them be more confident about expressing their thoughts.

- **Honest mistakes will happen**
  Accept this. When they do, managers must keep calm, remain supportive and be encouraging. Make mistakes teachable moments through constructive feedback. This helps individuals to better understand what led to the mistake and to know how to avoid it in the future.

SUGGESTED PHRASES

'Could you give me an example? We will work on it to make sure it isn't repeated.'

'Let's give you some more decision-based responsibilities to fix this. We can have a meeting in two months' time to reflect on whether this is working for you.'

Concerns over a lack of trust to make decisions

- **Delegate responsibility to the most suitable people**
  The people closest to the problem, who have all the facts, should make the decision, not the most senior or loudest, which so often happens. Where necessary, managers should work alongside these individuals to dig into the detail.
- **Avoid micromanagement**
  When managers are perceived to be controlling and/or nit-picking, it creates a culture of mistrust, decreases

management productivity, frustrates team members and inhibits success. When individuals feel empowered, it frees up management time, increases team effort and boosts overall engagement. Therefore, managers should avoid specifying every detail of how each task should be done. When they delegate, they should also voice their confidence in the team members.

- **Empowerment, not abandonment**
  Managers should make it clear that they are available for help and support, if required. While empowering the team is powerful because it gives them the opportunity to think for themselves and make decisions based on their own judgement, managers should clearly define boundaries and expectations on how much freedom they have.

- **Actively coach the team**
  Some decisions are more important than others, and these will be the ones that individuals will want to consult with their line managers on. When these questions come up, managers should first respond by asking individuals about their ideas, rather than simply providing their solutions or discussing how they would do it. They may need to advise them against doing something glaringly incorrect, but should be encouraging wherever they can. Once the action is complete, managers should provide appropriate and constructive feedback, discussing the full impact of the decisions.

- **Don't let the team be limited by a fear of making mistakes**
  If managers play the 'blame game' when mistakes are made, people will become overly cautious. When things

do go wrong, calmly discuss what can be learned from the mistake, how things might have been done differently and emphasize that this is a chance to learn and improve in the future. Let the team know that they should continue to step out of their comfort zone because it will develop their skills and benefit the whole organization.

• **Learn to trust the team**
Some managers will struggle to trust their team. In this case, they should work with a coach to see what is causing this issue and to come up with a plan to overcome it. Trusting others is an essential part of managing and leading people effectively. It is built through transparency, making meaningful choices for the team and empowering them to take part in decisions and actions.

SUGGESTED PHRASES

'I'd like to help you unpick why you might feel this way. Could you share some examples?'

Concerns over lack of resources to do the job well

• **Trust the judgement of team members**
The people who do the job know what they need to do the job well. Begin by asking members of the team:
  – What do you feel you need to do your job well?
  – What do you feel is missing?
  – What impact is it having on your job?

- **Be honest and open**

  Managers should make sure that team members under-stand the context of any constraints in providing re-sources. If access to what is needed is not immediately available, they can work with the team to find creative solutions. One of these solutions might be to explore whether resources or equipment are available elsewhere in the organization, which might be given or loaned. Some adaptability may be required, but the goal is to meet the needs of the team.

- **Match expectations and deadlines to available resources**

  If the team does not have the resources, they may not be able to complete the tasks that are set. Managers should provide regular check-ins and progress meetings to make sure expectations are aligned with what can be achieved.

SUGGESTED PHRASES

'I'd like to help you unpick why you might feel this way. Could you share some examples?'

Wellbeing

Great managers care about the wellbeing of everyone in their team. They are interested in their health, their family and their life. They notice if a team member is looking anxious or depressed and look to support and create a safe and protective working environment where people can be themselves.

When employees express unhappiness at work

- **Understand and embrace the six elements that lead to happiness at work**
  - reward and recognition
  - information sharing
  - empowerment
  - wellbeing
  - sense of pride
  - job satisfaction
- **Identify themes around what the team would like to improve their happiness**
  A simple survey which asks 'What would you change to be happier at work?' will almost certainly highlight key areas which are currently lacking. This is where any organization needs to begin.
- **Prioritize work/life balance and create an action plan**
  This plan should focus on empowering the team to take ownership, encouraging everyone to contribute to the conversation and putting in place measures so there is open and regular team feedback.
- **Pay close attention to remote workers**
  It is easy for remote workers to feel isolated and lonely. Organizations need to focus on ways to make everyone feel like a visible, involved member of the team.

SUGGESTED PHRASES

'Let's fix this together – we don't want anyone in the organization to feel this way.'

'What are the things we all enjoy about working together? If we know this, then we can do better.'

When workers don't feel happy or safe in the working environment

- **Understand the applicable health and safety regulations and check you are abiding by them**
  There is a legal duty to ensure, as far as reasonably practicable, the health, safety and welfare at work of employees under the Workplace (Health, Safety and Welfare) Regulations 1992. The Management of Health and Safety at Work Regulations 1999 (the Management Regulations) require organizations to assess and control risks to protect employees. Managers need to be clear on what they and their organization are accountable for when it comes to providing a safe place to work.
- **The health and safety of the team is the most important part of any manager's role**
  Managers must take responsibility for ensuring a good working environment for their team, overseeing elements such as space, cleanliness, lighting, ventilation, and adequate toilet, washing and changing facilities. If employees work outdoors, consideration needs to be given to weather, temperature (hot or cold) and sun exposure.
- **Keep risk assessments up to date**
  If new equipment or ways of working are introduced, appropriate risk assessments must be undertaken and consideration given to any health and safety implications.
- **All team members need to be aware of their own responsibilities for health and safety**
  Training in health and safety should be mandatory and an up-to-date record kept. Relevant training materials

should be easily accessible to all. Managers should appoint health and safety champions in each department and regularly meet with them to seek their ideas and identify any issues that may impact the team. All incidents should be logged in accordance with the organization's policies and near misses also noted, so remedies can be put in place to prevent future repeats.

- **Safety is not just about preventing injuries or disease**
  Organizations should be aware that creating a safe workplace extends to ensuring a positive working environment which encourages respect for everyone. Employee wellbeing, including the mental health of the team, is a priority.

SUGGESTED PHRASES

'Let's fix this together, we don't want anyone in the organization to feel this way.'

When workers feel anxious or depressed about work

- **Understand the scope of legal rights within your sector and check you are abiding by them**
  As a starting point, it is essential that managers are acquainted with the rights that are there to protect the mental health of all workers. These range from basic human rights, such as the right to freedom of expression and freedom of association, to health and safety legislation that protects the workforce from physical and psychological hazards. Key legislation to know about includes The Equality Act (2010) in England, Scotland

and Wales and the Disability Discrimination Act (1995, as amended) in Northern Ireland. Most people with ongoing mental health problems meet the definition of disability in the Equality Act (2010) and the Disability Discrimination Act (1995, as amended). This means they are protected from discrimination and harassment and entitled to reasonable adjustment to adapt their job.

· **Provide training**
All managers should be equipped with enough knowledge to spot the early signs of any issues, so they can provide the correct support. If necessary, training should be provided, so they can recognize common mental health issues such as stress, depression and anxiety, and know how to support staff in these circumstances.

· **Create a culture of open and positive communication about mental health**
This is crucial to remove any stigma and to encourage individuals to speak up. Organizations should also ensure that the team has access to the education and resources they need to cope if they experience any symptoms themselves, or need to support a colleague. Discrimination on the grounds of mental health needs to be as unacceptable as discrimination in relation to any other protected characteristic such as race, gender or sexual orientation. Staff should be encouraged to report any examples of discrimination or harassment they face on a personal level, or if they witness it elsewhere in the organization.

· **Provide mental health training and support to the team, where possible**
If there is an employee assistance programme in place, promote it and encourage individuals on the team to

use it where needed. Organizations should consider training some team members to become mental health first aiders.

- **Consider existing workload and wellbeing before increasing workloads**
  Team members may say 'yes' to additional tasks, even though they don't have the mental or physical capacity to do it. Managers should take responsibility for setting reasonable expectations and deadlines in line with the hours their team is already working, experience and skill. If workload is increased, managers should emphasize to the team that they appreciate the hard work they are putting in and make it very clear about tasks and their expectations. Often, it is the unknown that causes the most anxiety.

- **Reinforce the importance of taking breaks**
  Even if the issue of workload is not raised, all team members should be encouraged to take regular breaks. Managers should emphasize that they understand the importance of downtime.

- **Manager/team member relationships must stay friendly and professional**
  Managers should avoid oversharing or becoming friends with any individuals among their reports. This dynamic can lead others to suspect favouritism, which creates anxiety. Managers should focus on creating friendships with their peers and developing their own support system.

- **Give struggling team members the attention they need**
  Working with someone who is struggling can't be rushed. Managers should set aside at least 20 minutes of

clear time to speak with a colleague in this situation and give them their full attention. If applicable, time for a longer chat may need to be scheduled in. Thought should be given for where this takes place. Some people feel comfortable somewhere quiet and private, while others prefer something a bit more informal.

Managers need to develop active listening skills in a situation like this. They should maintain eye contact, unless the other person is clearly uncomfortable with this. They should sit facing them and respond to what is being said with nods and gestures, repeating what has been said to check they have understood. While they should ask direct and appropriate questions, they should be conscious of not probing beyond what someone is prepared to say.

Managers should be prepared with helpline numbers and web links in their phone which they can pass on to any team member who speaks about difficulties they are experiencing with their mental health. If there are concerns that this might be a crisis situation, they should immediately seek additional support and speak with the HR department if there is one.

SUGGESTED PHRASES

'How could we best support you to improve your wellbeing?'

'Have you identified any reasons for feeling this way? If you have, we will put safeguards in place to ensure the causes of stress are removed from your work life.'

Workers who question whether their employer cares for their wellbeing

- **Consider the wider impact of the way the organization operates**
  The environment, organization and its structure will affect the way the team operates. It is a useful exercise to consider every stage of the team's day and what they experience at each part of it. Think in terms of their mental health, physical health, financial wellbeing, stress management, emotional wellbeing, physical activity, social wellbeing and professional development.
- **What about the working environment?**
  It is crucial to provide a comfortable environment. Considerations here include the temperature, availability of appropriate equipment and, where possible, natural light.
- **Develop trusting relationships**
  As well as being available, approachable and actively listening to the team, managers should also encourage everyone around them to develop trusting relationships between one another. This is good for collaboration, too.
- **Show empathy**
  Giving and receiving thanks, celebrating successes and supporting colleagues who need help demonstrates your empathy with their needs and an understanding of how others see the world.
- **Communicate (a lot)**
  Organizations should include measures to allow everyone an input into decisions, or to share their views on fairness in pay, working hours and promotion

opportunities. On a day-to-day basis, managers should provide advance notice about changes to working hours.

- **Manage stress**

  Managers should pay close attention to the psychological impact of the work on individuals, ensuring people feel their work has purpose and is satisfying. If individuals are showing signs of stress, managers should work with them to discover the cause and alleviate problem areas. The goal is to offer as much choice and freedom in how they work as possible.

- **Address the physical aspect**

  Ascertain whether team members have enough time to rest. If they don't, there is a risk of physical and mental exhaustion. Where possible, encourage regular opportunities for movement for those who have roles which allow little room for physical activity. Give the team recommendations around good levels of physical activity, nutrition, hydration and peer support.

- **Promote programmes that encourage fitness and well-being**

  Managers should make available information about opportunities either within the organization or outside, which might include stop-smoking incentives, sponsored walks and mindfulness initiatives.

- **Examine opportunities for hybrid and flexible working**

  Rather than ushering everyone into the office, consider whether there is room for hybrid and flexible working. Often, it helps to think about it in terms of focusing on targets and results, rather than hours worked. This opens the way for managers to give team members the option to adjust working hours to what works best for them. In turn, it will increase the attractiveness of working with the organization, improve wellbeing, build trust and put it in a better position to attract and retain talent.

SUGGESTED PHRASES

'I'm sorry to hear that you're struggling with your wellbeing. Could you share a little more about why you might feel like this?'

'Apologies that you have felt this way – let's discuss some actions we can take together to fix this.'

Sense of pride

Great managers can explain to their team why their job is important to the department and the company as a whole, so that an individual feels they are doing something worthwhile and of importance. This helps them feel proud about where they work and what they do. At its best, an employee would tell friends and family what a great place they work at and even recommend that they should also get a job there.

When workers would absolutely not recommend that their friends and family work for their employer

- **Evaluate the employee proposition, how they are treated and the benefits and rewards on offer**
  This exercise will help an organization to identify any opportunities to improve, which will tip the balance

when it comes to recommending it as an employer to the outside world.

- **Be open to team input and opinions**
  Managers should take a genuine interest in their team's concerns, letting them know they are valued and that the organization cares about making sure the work they do is fulfilling.
- **Problems must be promptly addressed and resolved**
  If there is an issue that is damaging the team's view of the organization, it must be swiftly and effectively addressed.

SUGGESTED PHRASES

'Why do you think your family/friends wouldn't like this organization? Let's use this information to help us improve as a business.'

Workers who don't feel proud to work for their employer

- **Help teams understand the purpose of the organization**
  When managers are positive and proud of the organization where they work, it is infectious. It sets the tone and encourages others to take a pride in where they work. Individuals will go above and beyond expectations because doing their work makes them feel good.
- **Connect the dots by equating team contributions with organizational success**
  Managers should be specific in their praise when celebrating achievements. If, say, a team member handles a

difficult or unpleasant customer well, they should be praised for their patience and reminded of what a difference it has made since that customer will now no doubt return. Managers should not be shy about bragging about their team's achievements elsewhere in the organization, sharing credit where it is due and in particular with upper management.

- **Ensure team problems are addressed and resolved**
  Managers need to be alert to issues that may be damaging their team's pride in their work and take steps to remedy any problems as quickly as possible. If an individual's behaviour does not fit in with the organization's values, or is damaging to other team members, it needs to be dealt with immediately. For issues such as bullying, managers must meet with the perpetrator and put an end to the behaviour. This reinforces the standards expected.

- **Arrange regular team gatherings**
  If there is a natural weekly cycle, arrange a meeting at the end of the week; otherwise, pencil one in on a regular basis for an appropriate time. During the gathering managers should:
  - encourage the team to talk about what went well and any lessons for the week
  - recognize team and individual achievements in the time period
  - reaffirm the team's importance and finish on a high note

- **Take every opportunity to show everyone they are appreciated**
  Small gestures such as a hand-written note, an email or a thank you at the weekly meeting all have an outsized

impact. Small gifts, such as vouchers, are also a good way to show everyone that the efforts of their peers are recognized, while larger rewards, such as cash bonuses, can be tied to realistic performance goals.

SUGGESTED PHRASES

'Can I tell you my reason for feeling proud of the organization and then we will work together and find reasons that work for you?'

DEALING WITH DISCRIMINATION IN THE WORKPLACE WHEN RELATED TO RACE   Belton Flournoy, Managing Director, Global Business Consultancy

One of the first steps in addressing racial discrimination in the workplace is to seek to understand the problem you are trying to solve. Many organizations tend to start at the incident level and respond through policies and structural changes to reduce the number of incidents occurring. I would challenge organizations to focus on creating a cultural shift in the organization, one where leaders value diversity, rather than seeking racial assimilation.

I spend my days advising global companies how to get the most out of their technology investments. Some elements are the same for each project, such as the process for creating milestones, defining what success looks like, the tracking of finances and implementing a monitoring process to provide updates on the progression of activities. Organizations should leverage data for their diversity goals in the same way, enabling a more data-driven diversity strategy. This is not simply tracking ethnicity pay data, but also understanding racial trends among other key categories, such as hiring, employee tenure, regrettable departures and executive team/board representation.

Organizations should make sure they are aware of potential systemic issues. This requires defining key metrics that can better help to identify potential racial issues, rather than reports that contain general statistics. Look into how many complaints have been raised, regardless of outcome, not just those that come from 'approved' cases. Remember, diverse teams are not always reviewing these incidents as they come in. A high number of incidents that are not investigated could be a sign of a wider, systemic issue. One of the most important things for people is to feel like their concerns have been listened to; putting policies in place to ensure they are is not expensive.

The group of people who will be assessing the culture are important too. When the leadership is from a non-diverse group, in addition to a human resources or diversity and inclusion lead, it is possible to miss out on the 'lived experiences' of employees and what matters most to them. When someone has not truly experienced racism in their lifetime, it is extremely hard for them to understand the various emotions that exist as a result. While empathy can help, it is shielded by one of the more common things we hear: 'Is that really considered racist?'

Employee resource groups can be a valuable source of information when looking to understand the culture of your organization. If you do not have one yet, consider supporting the creation of one. If you do, find ways to work with them to understand the 'true racial culture' of your organization and how you can collaboratively work together to drive change. Work with human resources to understand feedback from exit interviews, and look to group similar responses.

An organization might try to address racial discrimination through 'unconscious bias training' and 'diverse hiring policies' but if the executive team do not believe that it will benefit the organization, a more appropriate place to start would be to educate leaders on the true benefits to be derived from a more inclusive workforce.

Worker concerns that they are not doing something worthwhile

- **Help everyone understand the purpose of the organization**
  An organization's core values are not just something that should be kept to leadership to strategize around. *Everyone* needs to know them and what they mean to their particular jobs. Managers should make it clear to each team member:
  - how their job supports the organization to succeed
  - why everyone should be involved in achieving these core values
  - why their commitment and wholehearted participation is crucial
- **Create high levels of engagement**
  Managers should create an environment where team members are encouraged to regularly submit suggestions and initiatives in line with the organization's purpose. This requires providing the means for open, two-way communication.

- **Demonstrate that roles have a broader purpose within society**
  Team members like it when their roles have a broader meaning, and a positive impact on the community, environment and even humankind. Managers should ensure they remind everyone this is the case and show them how.
- **Build meaningful and varied roles**
  Where possible, give individuals as much responsibility and variety of work within their capabilities. This will also encourage them to continually develop.

SUGGESTED PHRASES

'Can I tell you my reason for feeling like I do something worthwhile, and then we can work together to find reasons that work for you.'

Job satisfaction

Great managers are approachable. They are concerned about their team's career and personal development. They will actively coach, recommend training and help their reports get the right job to suit their skills and personalities.

Concerns that the organization is not well run

- **Ensure the team has accurate information about the organization's achievements**

This includes acknowledging where mistakes have been made and lessons learned.

- **Managers model behaviour**
  Managers should be positive about and proud of the organization, as this will set the tone for how everyone behaves at all levels.

> **SUGGESTED PHRASES**
>
> 'It would be great to have some feedback – we always want to improve as an organization.'

Concerns over personal and career development

- **Ensure each person understands their role**
  Managers should clearly spell out what each individual is expected to do and how their role fits into the success of the organization. This includes detailing expected standards of behaviour. They should also take the time to properly understand everyone's career goals and outline what needs to be done to accomplish them.
- **Create a culture of coaching and feedback**
  While it is crucial to focus on the positive, managers also need to share critical feedback, where necessary, to help people improve. If individuals know where they are going wrong, they can fix it in the future. If a manager is vague, or avoids addressing issues, it will not be to anyone's benefit.

- **Provide training and development for remote workers**
  To ensure remote workers feel visible, managers should give them the same development opportunities as office-based workers. This can be achieved via video calls for coaching and feedback, and by setting projects for individuals to work on, to build their experience and shape their abilities for future roles.
- **Let the team do their job**
  If the team is trained and they know the expectations and goals, they should be left to get on with it. Managers should remain available for support and provide supervision, but the more the team feels trusted and empowered, the better the job they are likely to do.
- **Hold regular meetings to discuss goals and performance**
  Development doesn't happen without accountability. Managers must provide regular check-in sessions where goals are reviewed and new ones set. They should use this opportunity to celebrate the successes and breakthroughs, and provide honest feedback on the actions that didn't go as well. Since each person will have a different learning style and pace, the feedback should be customized according to the individual.
- **Create career progression opportunities**
  Not every team member will have the potential, or even the desire, for promotion, but everyone will have the potential to develop. Managers should focus on providing stretch projects, being clear about the challenges and expectations around each one. They should listen to feedback to assess how motivated each individual is by the projects they are set, which will help share future stretch projects.

SUGGESTED PHRASES

'I would like to have a one-on-one conversation with you to tell me where you want to develop and we will build the next steps from there.'

'I would like to apologise for the lack of development meetings. We will arrange for them to happen for everyone in the next month and then make sure they happen every six months after that. We will try to make sure this remains a priority.'

'Let's start to create some goals that we both know will help your career progression.'

'Would you like to do a training course to ensure we are always allowing you to continue to go forward in your job?'

Concerns over relationships with managers

- **A manager's relationships with the team should be friendly and professional**
  These relationships should also be equitable. It can be very damaging to the team if one member appears to be favoured over the others, or treated as a personal friend. Managers should restrict friendships to peers.
- **Create a culture of trust**
  Treat the team with dignity and respect, and let them know that each one of them is a valued member of the department. If the team knows that their success matters to their managers, they will respect any development feedback and reward them by putting in the effort to improve.

- **Encourage team members to talk openly to one another**
  If one team member is complaining about another, managers should encourage them to raise the issue to their face. Left unchecked, it can create a toxic environment of gossip and recrimination.
- **Be open to opinions**
  When managers take a genuine interest in team concerns, it signals that they are valued and that the organization wants to make sure that the work they do is fulfilling.

SUGGESTED PHRASES

'I'm sorry you feel that way. Let's have a one-on-one conversation to discuss actions to improve this.'

'Would you be interested in a team-building exercise so we can improve our relationships?'

'Please would you give me some constructive feedback on how I can improve our relationship? It can be anonymous, if people are more comfortable with that.'

Workers who say they don't enjoy their job

- **Identify what would help the team enjoy their jobs more**
  Managers should engage with the team to ask them to share their thoughts on what could be done to get more out of their working day on a personal level.
- **Be mindful of team members who deal with distressing situations**
  In this situation, organizations should look to design some relief into the role and also ensure the correct

supervision is in place to protect employees from the worst impact of their situation.

- **Encourage team members to take responsibility for their own happiness**
  We all play a role in the amount of enjoyment we get out of our working day. Team members need to be helped to think in this way.

- **Managers model behaviour**
  Once more, managers should take responsibility for being as open, fun and engaging as possible. If necessary, they should develop measures to manage their own stress and create their own support network.

> **SUGGESTED PHRASES**
>
> 'What aspects of your job are you feeling unhappy about? We can try to alleviate some/all of these to make sure you feel happier about this job.'

Concerns over being treated with respect

- **Lead by example**
  Managers must always be respectful of the preferences, beliefs and opinions of others. They should avoid swearing and create an environment that is comfortable and inclusive for all. During meetings, they should make sure their comments are constructive, on topic and respectful, and never interrupt others.

- **Observe and be alert to behaviour between team members**
  Managers who see or hear about disrespectful behaviour should speak up and take appropriate action. If it is ignored, or seen to be tolerated, it will damage the culture.

- **Managers should acknowledge everyone they meet**
  This can be as simple as a smile, or a greeting as people arrive at work, and saying 'thank you' with sincerity. Managers should also vocalize their gratitude and give regular encouragement to the team to show they value their contributions.

- **Acknowledge mistakes**
  We all make them. When a manager does, they should take responsibility and show there is a plan to correct it. The mere act of saying 'sorry' without making excuses is courageous and shows a commitment to colleagues and the organization.

- **Respond in a timely manner to contact from team members**
  If a manager replies promptly to calls and emails, it shows their colleagues that they are valued, while also ensuring useful information is communicated and shared. This is a signal of trust and confidence in the team.

- **Be reliable**
  If a manager says they are going to do something, they should keep their word and follow through. If necessary, they can set up a system of task lists and reminders, as well as avoiding distractions that make it too easy to lose sight of deadlines. Confidential information should always be kept strictly confidential.

SUGGESTED PHRASES

'I'm sorry you feel that way – let's have a one-on-one conversation to discuss actions to improve this.'

Afterword

If you take a look around your kitchen, the chances are you'll find all sorts of high-tech gadgets. There may be anything from ice makers to high-pressure hoses to rinse off dirty dishes, to taps which instantly dispense boiling water. Once upon a time, these gadgets were the preserve of high-end restaurant kitchens, but for many of us they are now part of our day-to-day life. I see many parallels here with what we are seeing today in the corporate world. Even just a few years ago, your happiness at work and your development was left to the HR professionals. Their role was to make sure everyone properly understood their jobs, were supported with the training they needed and their wellbeing catered for. It's a huge remit and this may be why it has been achieved with varying results. Things are changing, though. The tools and ideas covered in this book are the same ones that the HR department used to be responsible for. This means, quite rightly, that employees can be empowered to manage their own development and the whole organization can become involved in Happy Economics. Now you have the tools, you can make your corporate happiness plan and make your business a genuinely happy place to be.

It is important that everyone gets involved, too. At WorkL, we uniquely offer all employees, not just managers, feedback on staff surveys. This book has talked a lot about how leaders and managers play a pivotal role in shaping the work environment. It is in their gift to create a trusting, positive and supportive workplace culture that contributes significantly to the generation of pride among staff. It is they that will ensure that team members are well informed about aspects of the organization's performance and challenges and who will encourage autonomy in their work and a healthy work/life balance. It is also up to the individual. We all bear responsibility for our own happiness. We spend so much of our life at work that it's important we find the right job, get on with our manager and our colleagues and enjoy the social aspects of our working life. That's so much better than just thinking, 'I can't wait for the next 30 years to pass by so I can retire.'

I can't help thinking of a conversation I had with the chairman of a once much-loved legacy retail brand which was really struggling. He told me that one of his most pressing problems was that his stores were populated by far too many long-serving members of staff who, frankly, didn't want to be there. However, they'd been there so long and built up such a store of perks and benefits that they didn't want to go. It wasn't helping his recovery efforts at all.

'What I'd really love to do is to find a way to say to those people, have you thought about working elsewhere, since you are clearly not happy working here?' he mused.

He was exactly right.

When I entered the working world, it was very paternalistic. The attitude from employers was '*We'll* decide on what's best for you, what you are going to learn and when you're going to move jobs.' Things have changed in this, and indeed all other aspects of our lives. Individuals have assumed responsibility for their life, what they do, who they marry and whether they have kids. It is the same when it comes to work. We get to decide where we work and how we work. It's got to be our choice and we've got to take control. People who take control are happier, rather than feeling that everything is being done *to* them. This is why one of the key aspects to what we're trying to do at WorkL is to give people that power to make the right informed choices. We'll help people measure whether they are happy at work. We'll even tell them what it is about their job that's making them feel either more or less happy when compared to other people, and if necessary find them a job in a company where we think they're going to fit in better. But, when all is said and done, individuals need to get involved and make an active choice to be happy, rather than coming home each day and moaning about their jobs.

Of course, as we have shown here, workplace happiness is not just beneficial to the individual. The extra discretionary effort that comes about as a result also gives a multitude of advantages to the employer, from increased productivity, improved retention rates, more innovation and creativity and reduced absenteeism. The list goes on. As a consequence, businesses are better and the economy is better, too. Happiness really does make the world a better place. It really is in all our best interests to think about happiness.

I believe that in the months and years to come, happiness will gain substantial importance as a workplace metric (and it is about time too). It's not just because this is something that will make all the difference in recruiting and retaining Gen Z talent, although it will. In an increasingly hybrid and tech-reliant world, personal relationships will be valued ever more highly. It is inevitable that people will feel socially distant and seek out a deeper, more meaningful bond with their colleagues. People will gravitate towards workplaces that help them feel at ease and valued for their input. Employers can future proof their businesses by understanding what it is that makes their teams happy and then investing time and resources into human capital, putting this crucial metric on a par with, or even ahead of, social and financial capital.

As the evidence we have presented shows, happy teams give extra discretionary effort. That extra effort turns in to commercial out-performance. That's good for the employee, the organization and society.

That's Happy Economics.

> Visit HappyEconomics.com to see where your organization ranks in the global workplace happiness list.

Notes

Introduction

1   R Kennedy. Speech, 1968, Clinton Whitehouse Archives, nd.
    clintonwhitehouse4.archives.gov/PCSD/Publications/TF_Reports/
    linkage-chap4.html (archived at https://perma.cc/N83P-6EW6)
2   R Easterlin and K O'Connor. The Easterlin Paradox, IZA Institute,
    2020. docs.iza.org/dp13923.pdf (archived at https://perma.cc/69V2-
    HXG4)
3   BBC. Plan to measure happiness 'not woolly' – Cameron, BBC, 2010.
    www.bbc.co.uk/news/uk-11833241 (archived at https://perma.cc/
    F7TQ-XHXC)
4   J-E De Neve. Why wellbeing matters and how to improve it, Said
    Business School, University of Oxford, 2020. www.sbs.ox.ac.uk/
    oxford-answers/why-wellbeing-matters-and-how-improve-it (archived at
    https://perma.cc/TR74-Y64Z)
5   WorkL. WorkL global workplace report 2024, Flipsnack, 2024. www.
    flipsnack.com/workl/workl-s-global-workplace-report-2024-press-
    version.html (archived at https://perma.cc/RE82-PAQF)
6   P Pell. What you need to recruit and retain Gen Z, Abode, 2023. www.
    abodehr.com/blog/what-you-need-to-recruit-and-retain-gen-z (archived
    at https://perma.cc/3FWT-HCRD)
7   T Brower. Gen Z are quitting in droves, Forbes, 2023. www.forbes.com/
    sites/tracybrower/2023/09/24/gen-zs-are-quitting-in-droves-6-best-ways-
    to-retain-them (archived at https://perma.cc/5UZ9-SCLP)

Chapter Two: The facts

1   Aon Hewitt. 2015 trends in global employee engagement, Aon, 2015.
    www.aon.com/attachments/human-capital-consulting/2015-Trends-in-
    Global-Employee-Engagement-Report.pdf (archived at https://perma.
    cc/3VL2-TCV9)

Part One: Six steps towards workplace happiness

1   Gallup. The benefits of employee engagement, Gallup, 2013.
     www.gallup.com/workplace/236927/employee-engagement-drives-
     growth.aspx (archived at https://perma.cc/LB83-LEH9)

Chapter Six: Wellbeing

1   B Daisley. Gen Z can handle stress – in fact they're brave enough to say
     it's unacceptable, *The Guardian*, 2022. www.theguardian.com/
     commentisfree/2022/oct/12/gen-z-stress-resilience (archived at https://
     perma.cc/3942-NENM)

2   Gallup. State of the global workplace: 2023 report, Gallup, 2023. www.
     gallup.com/workplace/349484/state-of-the-global-workplace.aspx
     (archived at https://perma.cc/M27D-AFSM)

3   CIPD. Health and wellbeing at work, CIPD, 2022. www.cipd.org/
     globalassets/media/comms/news/ahealth-wellbeing-work-report-2022_
     tcm18-108440.pdf (archived at https://perma.cc/VFA4-3TQF)

4   In writing this piece, Dr Luke Fletcher drew on his published academic
     research on topics related to anxiety, including:
     N Babu, L Fletcher, S Pichler and P Budhwar. What's trust got to do
     with it? Examining trust in leadership, psychological capital and
     employee wellbeing in a cross-national context during COVID-19,
     European Management Review, 2023. Doi: 10.1111/emre.12561
     (archived at https://perma.cc/XS8A-ZDWF)
     L Fletcher. The everyday experience of engagement: What matters most?
     Human Resource Development Quarterly, 2017, 28 (4), 451–79. Doi:
     10.1002/hrdq.21288 (archived at https://perma.cc/87T5-N342)
     L Fletcher. How can personal development lead to increased
     engagement? The roles of meaningfulness and perceived line manager
     relations, *The International Journal of Human Resource Management*,
     2019, 30 (7), 1203–26. Doi: 10.1080/09585192.2016.1184177
     L Fletcher and K Schofield. Facilitating meaningfulness in the
     workplace: A field intervention study, *The International Journal of
     Human Resource Management*, 2021, 32 (14), 2975–3003. Doi:
     10.1080/09585192.2019.1624590

L Fletcher, K Alfes and D Robinson. The relationship between perceived training and development and employee retention: the mediating role of work attitudes, *The International Journal of Human Resource Management*, 2018, 29 (18), 2701–28. Doi: 10.1080/09585192. 2016.1262888.

L Fletcher, C Bailey and M Gilman. Fluctuating levels of personal role engagement within the working day: A multilevel study, *Human Resource Management Journal*, 2018, 28 (1), 128–47. Doi: 10.1111/1748-8583.12168 (archived at https://perma.cc/5TEC-HNVB)

E Lysova, L Fletcher and S El-Baroudi. What enables us to better experience our work as meaningful? The importance of awareness and the social context, *Human Relations*, 2023, 76 (8), 1226–55. Doi: 10.1177/00187267221094243 (archived at https://perma.cc/6QJK-BPRX)

S Pichler, W Casper, L Fletcher and N Babu. Adaptation in work and family roles link support to mental health during a pandemic, *Journal of Occupational and Organizational Psychology*, 2023 96 (4), 725–53. Doi: 10.1111/joop.12452 (archived at https://perma.cc/3KG9-RZN4)

L Fletcher, M Carter and J Lyubovnikova. Congruency of resources and demands and their effects on staff turnover within the English healthcare sector, *Journal of Occupational and Organizational Psychology*, 2018, 91 (3), 688–96. Doi: 10.1111/joop.12214 (archived at https://perma.cc/2KQB-NMCK)

Chapter Eight: Job satisfaction

1 Glassdoor Team. How to calculate your cost per hire, Glassdoor, 2020. www.glassdoor.co.uk/employers/blog/calculate-cost-per-hire (archived at https://perma.cc/HBQ3-GC9Y)

2 S Bessalel. LinkedIn 2024 most in-demand skills: Learn the skills companies need most, LinkedIn, 2024. www.linkedin.com/business/learning/blog/top-skills-and-courses/most-in-demand-skills (archived at https://perma.cc/9VZJ-W8RY)

3 OECD. OECD skills outlook 2023: Skills for a resilient green and digital transition, OECD, 2023. www.oecd.org/education/oecd-skills-outlook-e11c1c2d-en.htm (archived at https://perma.cc/7SNP-KWHQ)

4   CIPD. More work needed to improve employee development and career
     progression, CIPD, 2016. www.cipd.org/uk/about/news/improve-
     employee-development-and-career-progression (archived at https://
     perma.cc/UMN6-UJZS)

Chapter Nine: The vital role of good leadership

1   CMI. Taking responsibility: Why UK plc needs better managers, CMI,
     2023. www.managers.org.uk/wp-content/uploads/2023/10/CMI_BMB_
     GoodManagment_Report.pdf (archived at https://perma.cc/BR98-34R4)
2   M Race. More than a fifth of UK adults not looking for work, BBC,
     2024. www.bbc.com/news/business-68534537 (archived at https://
     perma.cc/7FHZ-QKUS)

Chapter Eleven: A word on culture

1   J Parker. 'When a flower doesn't bloom, you fix the environment
     in which it grows, not the flower, Julie Parker, 2019.
     julieparkerpracticesuccess.com/when-a-flower-doesnt-bloom-you-fix-
     the-environment-in-which-it-grows-not-the-flower (archived at https://
     perma.cc/K93R-XXYG)

Chapter Twelve: Troubleshooting

1   A De Smet. Some employees are destroying value. Others are building it.
     Do you know the difference? McKinsey, 2023. www.mckinsey.com/
     capabilities/people-and-organizational-performance/our-insights/
     some-employees-are-destroying-value-others-are-building-it-do-you-
     know-the-difference (archived at https://perma.cc/D4XL-FECK)
2   E Field. Middle managers are the heart of your company, McKinsey,
     2023. www.mckinsey.com/capabilities/people-and-organizational-
     performance/our-insights/middle-managers-are-the-heart-of-your-
     company (archived at https://perma.cc/2T7T-YSTU)

Index

Looking for another book?

Explore our award-winning books from global business experts in General Business

Scan the code to browse

www.koganpage.com/general-business